# BOWLING

## Steps to Success

### Second Edition

**Robert H. Strickland, MS**
Duncanville, Texas

**Human Kinetics**

**Library of Congress Cataloging-in-Publication Data**

Strickland, Robert.
    Bowling : steps to success / Robert H. Strickland. -- 2nd ed.
    p.      cm. -- (Steps to success activity series)
    Includes bibliographical references (p.  ).
    ISBN 0-87322-581-3
    1. Bowling.   I. Title.   II. Series.
  GV903.S76   1996
  794.6--dc20                                                                      95-50384
                                                                                   CIP

ISBN: 0-87322-581-3

Human Kinetics books are available at special discounts for bulk purchase. Special editions or book excerpts can also be created to specification. For details, contact the Special Sales Manager at Human Kinetics.

**Developmental Editor:** Judy Patterson Wright, PhD; **Assistant Editor:** John Wentworth; **Editorial Assistant:** Jennifer Hemphill; **Copyeditor:** Tom Taylor; **Proofreader:** Jacqueline Seebaum; **Typesetter and Layout Artist:** Kathleen Boudreau-Fuoss; **Text Designer:** Keith Blomberg; **Cover Designer:** Jack Davis; **Photographer (cover):** Will Zehr; **Illustrator:** Raneé Rogers and Emily Mann; **Mac Illustrator:** Jennifer Delmotte; **Printer:** United Graphics

**Instructional Designer for the Steps to Success Activity Series:** Joan N. Vickers, EdD, University of Calgary, Calgary, Alberta, Canada

Printed in the United States of America      10  9  8

**Human Kinetics**
Web site: www.HumanKinetics.com

*United States:* Human Kinetics, P.O. Box 5076, Champaign, IL 61825-5076
800-747-4457
e-mail: humank@hkusa.com

*Canada:* Human Kinetics, 475 Devonshire Road, Unit 100, Windsor, ON N8Y 2L5
800-465-7301 (in Canada only)
e-mail: orders@hkcanada.com

*Europe:* Human Kinetics, 107 Bradford Road, Stanningley
Leeds LS28  6AT, United Kingdom
+44 (0) 113 255 5665
e-mail: hk@hkeurope.com

*Australia:* Human Kinetics, 57A Price Avenue, Lower Mitcham, South Australia 5062
08  8277 1555
e-mail: liahka@senet.com.au

*New Zealand:* Human Kinetics, P.O. Box 105-231, Auckland Central
09-523-3462
e-mail: hkp@ihug.co.nz

# CONTENTS

# PREFACE

When I was learning how to bowl (and even long into a successful competitive bowling career), I often found myself in situations that would have been much easier if I had known certain facts and how to perform certain skills—how to execute a movement, how to practice more productively, and how to organize my thoughts and actions for success during competition, just to name a few. Because standard texts provided few answers, my needs were unfulfilled until I got a tip from an experienced bowler, or stumbled onto a successful technique after hours, days, weeks, even months of frustrating trial and error.

This second edition of *Bowling: Steps to Success* is an updated collection of facts, tips, strategies, and techniques arranged in a sequence to enable you to learn easily, retain the lessons, and apply your bowling skills effectively when you need them—during practice or in a game. You will become skilled at executing a free-pendulum swing, essential to the four-step delivery. You will learn effective strike- and spare-targeting principles to follow, as well as mental practice skills designed to improve both your bowling form and your scoring potential. The easy-to-difficult drill arrangement will not only help you ingrain the feel of efficient movements but also troubleshoot your own performance by comparing your movement to how the correct ones feel. Many of the drills utilize a buddy system so you and your lane mates can help each other learn quickly. Each drill helps you pace your practice to best fit your skill level, and lists those details most important for success. The drills within later learning steps help you adjust to different lane conditions and different competitive situations. I hope you enjoy your steps-to-success journey.

Make *Bowling: Steps to Success* your constant companion during practice. If you are a beginner, use it to learn correct form and techniques from the start. If you are already a skilled bowler, use it systematically to help you break out of slumps and eliminate bad habits, while filling the holes in your knowledge and simplifying your bowling form.

Thanks to Wilson G. "Bill" Taylor for certain techniques included in this book. Our many discussions and workouts helped me understand and feel elements of bowling form more deeply. His teaching strategies, which make use of the extension setup, the assisted balance arm, the finish, and the footwork drill, are major contributions to *Bowling: Steps to Success* and to students of bowling. Without his assistance, I could not have written this book.

Thanks to my wife, Sue, for her loving support, for posing for many of the photographs for use by the illustrator, and for critically evaluating the manuscript. Her keen ideas, especially those concerning the grip, contributed immeasurably to the practical nature of these lessons. Thanks to Jim and Cina Goodwin, then proprietors of Circle Bowl, Dallas, Texas, now publishers of *Stars and Strikes* bowling magazine, for allowing us to use their facility as staging for the picture shoots. Thanks to Pete Moore, member of the Dallas Bowling Association Hall of Fame, for the loan of special camera equipment, for his always helpful suggestions, and for proofreading the galleys. Thanks to David Brewster, Myra Lachausse, Dr. Will Powers, and Manuel San Miguel for posing for photographs for use by the illustrator, and for their helpful suggestions on how to improve them. Dr. Powers' concepts, including his "Mental Toughness Routine," added greatly to the effectiveness of the section on mental discipline. Thanks to Glenn Scifres for suggesting the term "low maintenance game." Lastly, and most sincerely, thanks to all of our students for helping Sue and myself learn and refine our teaching techniques, and for giving us a reason to continue teaching.

# THE STEPS TO SUCCESS STAIRCASE

Get ready to climb a staircase—one that will lead you to become an accomplished bowler. You cannot leap to the top; you get there by climbing one step at a time.

Each of the 10 steps you will take is an easy transition from the one before. The first few steps of the staircase provide a solid foundation of basic skills and concepts. As you progress, you will learn how to make strikes consistently, convert spares, prepare mentally, and adapt to various game situations. As you near the top of the staircase, you will become more confident in your ability to be successful in practice, league, and tournament play.

Familiarize yourself with this section, as well as "The Sport of Bowling" and the "Selecting Your Equipment" sections, for an orientation and to understand how to set up your practice sessions around the steps (chapters).

Follow the same sequence each step of the way:

1. Read the explanations of what is covered in the step, why the step is important, and how to execute or perform the step's focus, which may be on basic skills, concepts, tactics, or a combination of the three.
2. Follow the numbered illustrations showing exactly how to position your body to execute each basic skill successfully. There are three general parts to each skill: preparation (getting into a starting position), execution (performing the skill that is the focus of the step), and recovery (reaching a finish position or following through to starting position).
3. Look over the common errors that may occur and the recommendations for how to correct them.
4. The drills help you improve your skills through repetition and purposeful practice. Read the directions, the Success Goal, and the Success Check for each drill. Practice accordingly and record your results. You need to meet the Success Goal of each drill before moving on to practice the next one, because the drills are arranged in an easy-to-difficult progression. This sequence is designed specifically to help you achieve continual success. If the basic instructions are either too easy or too difficult, see the sections "To Increase Difficulty" and "To Decrease Difficulty," and follow the directions most appropriate for your skill level.
5. As soon as you can reach all the Success Goals for one step, you are ready for a trained observer—such as your teacher, coach, or trained partner—to evaluate your basic skill technique against the Keys to Success. This is a qualitative or subjective evaluation of your basic technique or form, because using correct form can enhance your performance. There is a blank scoresheet for recording practice games in the appendix.
6. Repeat these procedures for each of the 10 Steps to Success. Then rate yourself according to the directions in the "Rating Your Progress" section.

Good luck on your step-by-step journey to developing your bowling skills, building confidence, experiencing success, and having fun!

# THE SPORT OF BOWLING

Bowling is at least 7,000 years old and can be traced to Egypt, where archaeologists unearthed stone balls and pins from a child's grave site. The next 5,000 years of bowling's history is lost to the ages.

In third-century Germany, bowling was a religious rite. At that time, Germans carried clubs called *Kegels* for protection. At one end of the church cloister a kegel would be set up to symbolize a heathen. Transgressors were required to roll a ball at it from the other end of the cloister. If the bowler (*kegler*) knocked over the kegel, he was said to have killed the heathen and was honored at a post-session banquet. However, a bowler failing to knock over the kegel was encouraged to seek spiritual fortification in church.

For the next thousand years, Germans bowled at clusters of 3 to 17 pins; 9 emerged as the most popular number. Play was commonly conducted on such diverse surfaces as clay, slate, and cinders, with the wooden surface first appearing in Holland and Switzerland. The playing surface (lane) of this time was approximately 1 foot wide.

Ninepin bowling spread to France, England, and Spain at about the same time, but with varied pin arrangements and widely diverse pin dimensions. The French had *quilles*, and the English had *skittles* and long-bowling, the forerunner of the modern game of bowling.

In England, bowling was a commoner's sport, the first public establishment being opened in London in the 15th century. The word *alley* became associated with pin bowling establishments, and bowling became more closely identified with tavern life. It was with this image that bowling came to America with the Dutch colonists.

Allen (1986) divides the evolution of bowling in America into four general time periods based upon the way participation was organized, the establishment of standards, and the localization of control. During the *developmental era* (1837-1875) bowling grew as a regular outdoor family activity for German immigrant social groups.

Eventually ninepin bowling moved indoors to ethnic cultural centers in which persons of similar background could enjoy food, drink, and recreational activities together. In 1840, America's first commercial indoor ninepin bowling establishment, the Knickerbocker Alleys, opened in Manhattan. This venture was successful, primarily because it served New York's large German population. Soon the outward enthusiasm of these people for bowling attracted other Americans to the sport.

Bowling continued to draw gamblers and hustlers; bowling enthusiasts waged continuous battles against local authorities who tried to ban bowling activity as a way to eliminate gambling, the idle use of time, and drinking. It is believed that the addition of a 10th pin to the pin arrangement was a tactic to circumvent an 1837 Connecticut ban of public ninepin bowling.

As public bans on leisure activities became more frequent, bowling groups answered the challenge by forming clubs, legally protected as long as they were appropriately licensed and formed for the common good of the members. During the *club era* (1875–1895), the permissive club environment provided a way for serious enthusiasts to shape the development of bowling in America. Bowling's continued existence was assured within the confines of the club, but the chaotic state of playing rules and standards left the future of large-scale competitive bowling uncertain. Bowling took many forms: bowlers of the east played by different rules from bowlers of the west; some bowled ninepins, whereas others bowled tenpins.

During these years, the maximum score was usually 200, with three balls allowed per *frame* (each attempt to knock down a full setup of pins) and 10 frames making up one game. In some areas, a bowler started with 200 points, and points were deducted with each roll of the ball, the objective being to be the first to reach zero. Fallen pins were either left on the lane or swept off before the next ball was rolled. Further, the size and weight of balls and pins varied greatly, and there were no standards concerning lane specifications.

Uniform rules and standards were absolutely vital for the growth of bowling and the beginning of nationwide competition. Bowling clubs formed umbrella organizations for the purpose of imposing rules and standards to which all participants could adhere. These governing bodies were not cohesive enough to survive, but each made some contribution to the overall goal of standardization.

The first regulatory group, the National Bowling Association (NBA), made up of members of several clubs, appeared in 1875. The NBA formulated rules about ball size, playing procedures, and lane dimensions. In 1890 the American Bowling League (ABL), successor to the NBA, standardized pin size and eliminated the third ball from the frame, but left the maximum possible score at 200.

The *competitive era* (1895-1961) featured the most remarkable growth of competitive bowling. It began with the formation of the American Bowling Congress (ABC), with which most league bowlers are familiar today. In 1895 this body agreed upon the present method of scoring with 300 as a maximum score, giving the bowler more room for improvement. It also agreed upon the current 12-inch center-to-center spacing of pins, and initiated a program of lane inspection to ensure consistency with adopted specifications.

The ABC also started a yearly tournament to promote the sport and allow bowlers from all parts of the nation to compete with each other under standardized conditions. Two such tournaments exist today: the ABC Tournament for men and the WIBC (Women's International Bowling Congress) Tournament for women. Each features scratch competition in singles, doubles, and five-member team events.

As bowling began to provide great fame and monetary reward, skilled bowlers were often featured in match-game competition. They would barnstorm through the country with their financial backers, or take on all challengers in their own (*home*) establishments, which were often filled to capacity. Because these matches involved wagering, the bigger the crowd, the more intense the betting action. A big draw was advantageous to the proprietor, who sold more food and drink; to the traveling star and his group, who were paid for the appearance; and to all gamblers, who stood better chances to diversify their bets in a larger crowd.

Naturally there was a tremendous commercial advantage in being designated "the best bowler in America" or "the best bowler in the world." Many claimed to be so, and such claims became so careless and widespread that the *challenge-match system* became a way to determine who really was the best. Challenge matches followed most of the several large tournaments held around the country, but there were no formal schedules like those we see in professional bowling today. Skilled bowlers simply participated in as many of these tournaments as they could. The person with the best winning record had the right to claim the national match-game championship or to challenge the current champion to a series of match games, during which the title could change hands. The winner of the challenge match was then obliged to defend his title against other worthy opponents.

The challenge method was discarded in favor of the All-Star tournament, for which participants had to qualify through a system of local and state competition. The All-Star was later joined by a similar tournament, the World's Invitational, to which the best bowlers were invited. Women's divisions were added later. These tournaments served nicely to determine the best in the *field* (total group of participants) by running bowlers through the difficult paces of a 100-game format!

Because of extensive television exposure in the late 1950s and early 1960s, bowling experienced a sharp rise in popularity with people of all ages. This bowling boom accounted for the appearance of many large bowling centers around the country, where bowling was given its finishing touches as a full-blown family recreation. The Professional Bowlers Association (PBA) was founded in 1958, emphasizing scratch singles competition for skilled bowlers. The PBA's continuing television coverage, and that of the Ladies' Professional Bowlers Tour (LPBT), keep bowling in the public eye.

The *commercial era* (1961 to the present) is characterized by the deemphasis of the sport image of bowling in favor of a recreational image. The bowling industry feels that its interests are best served by promoting bowling as an easily learned recreational activity. This attitude is reflected in the active marketing of high-velocity pins, the increased elasticity of bowling balls, and the conditioning of lane surfaces to promote high scoring. The game of the present era, although less demanding in accuracy than the game of the 1940s and 1950s, is still America's most popular communal sport.

## Conduct

*Courtesy* and *sportsmanship* are essential for all competitors to enjoy peak performance! Bowlers must work together to respect the right of each participant to be as good as his or her ability will allow. Therefore, courtesy and sportsmanship are everyone's responsibility.

Here are some ways you can help yourself and others:

1. *Respect the equipment.* Do not *loft* the ball, tossing it far out onto the lane surface; it will make a pockmark in the lane. Do not kick the ball return. Do not roll a second ball until your first one has returned; you may find yourself liable for any damages that occur to expensive equipment. Also, do not use another person's ball without permission. Keep all personal items, especially bowling balls and bags, off the seats and out of any traffic area.

2. *Respect the valuable time of your teammates and the proprietor* by being ready when it is your turn to bowl. Remain in and around the settee area until it is your turn to bowl; meet the person who bowls before you as he or she is stepping off the approach. During practice, take only one practice ball—not a whole frame—at a time. Then step aside, allowing the next person his or her practice ball. If you wait to roll a second ball, you deprive the bowlers on your pair of lanes (including yourself) of approximately one third of the total practice time.

3. *Always allow the bowlers around you every chance to concentrate* on each shot. Yield to the bowler on your immediate left or right if he or she is ready to bowl. Do not distract anyone in the setup. Be quiet in and around your settee area. Avoid standing on the approach next to any bowler (an exception is made for anyone working out with an instructor or a partner in a class setting). Control your emotions by confining your movements to your approach, making no animated gestures when returning from the foul line, and making no sudden noises at any time.

4. *Create a positive atmosphere.* Avoid wasting time on the approach, making excuses for poor bowling, bragging about your achievements, laughing at or berating others, needling any opponent, or using loud or vulgar language. Avoid saying anything negative or anxiety-causing to anyone—especially when he or she is returning from making a bad shot. Give no advice to anyone, unless he or she has asked for advice.

## General Safety Tips

The bowling environment presents two major dangers to the untrained bowler—falling down and being hit. Falling down can be minimized by making sure there are no foreign substances on your shoes or on the approach. Follow these guidelines:

- Never apply powder or ashes to help you slide.
- Always keep food and drinks out of the bowling area.
- Never step beyond the foul line; you might track lane dressing onto the approach.
- Never bowl in street shoes.
- Always check the bottoms of your shoes before bowling if you have walked out of the settee area for any reason.
- Watch out for being hit with, or hitting someone else with, a bowling ball.
- Always look around you to see whether anyone is taking practice swings.
- Be careful with your own practice swings; always know how much room you have for making your movements. A good idea is to take practice swings or slides only on the approach and in the direction of the pins.
- Pick up your ball only on its sides, with both hands, and only after it has come to a stop on the ball return. You can avoid smashing your fingers if you look down at your ball as you pick it up with both hands (see Figures 1a and 1b).

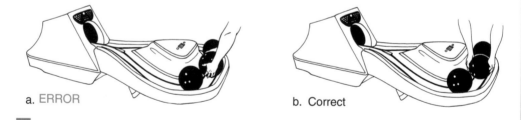

a. ERROR                                          b. Correct

**Figure 1** In picking up a bowling ball (a) improper technique risks smashed fingers, and (b) proper technique ensures safety.

Finally, heed these two warnings (they seem obvious, but you'd be surprised how often they occur!):

- Never trigger the pinsetting machine to operate if someone is working on it.
- Never roll a ball toward the pins if someone is working on the pinsetter or if the pins are not fully exposed and ready for the ball to be rolled.

## How a Game Is Played

Tenpin bowling is a game played by *delivering* (rolling) a ball 27 inches in circumference (about 8-1/2 inches diameter) down an *alley*, or *lane*, 42 inches (39 boards) wide. The ball rolls 60 feet toward a *rack* (formation) of 10 pins. The pins, each 15 inches high, are set in an equilateral triangular formation, the center of one pin 12 inches from the next (see Figures 2 and 3). The primary objective is to *strike*—to knock down all of the pins with one delivery of the ball. If a strike does not occur, the secondary objective is to *spare*—to knock down all of the pins left standing after the first delivery with a second delivery of the ball. A *cumulative score* is kept.

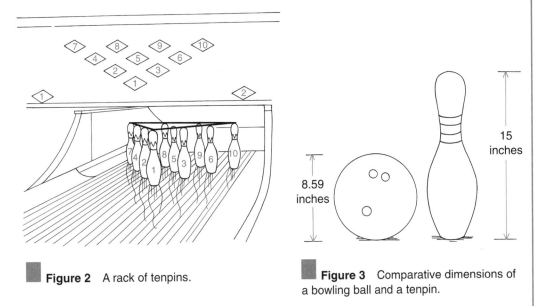

**Figure 2**   A rack of tenpins.

**Figure 3**   Comparative dimensions of a bowling ball and a tenpin.

The bowler takes an *approach* (movements from the setup to the release of the ball) within an area 15 feet by 42 inches, also called the *approach* or the *runway*. While delivering the ball, the bowler must not cross the *foul line*, the line that separates the approach from the lane proper. If the foul line is crossed, the delivery is declared illegal, and any pins knocked down count as zero. The bowler should also avoid rolling the ball into one of the 9-inch-wide *gutters*, or *channels*, on either side of the lane (see Figure 4). Pins knocked down by a ball coming out of the channel do not count. See the current year's edition of the *American Bowling Congress Constitution, Specifications, Rules and Suggested League Rules Manual* for lane construction specifications.

## Types of Game Play

There are several game contexts. The one in which beginners usually bowl is *open play*, self-paced, nonstructured bowling, not overseen (or *sanctioned*) by any organization, for example, someone dropping in to bowl a few games during the lunch hour. Open play may be recreational enjoyment (the bowler uses the game for relaxation), or serious practice (featuring intense concentration on technique).

The opposite of open play is *competitive* bowling. It is divided into league and tournament competition, both of which are typically overseen by some governing organization, such as the ABC (men), the WIBC (women), or the Young American Bowling Alliance (YABA, for youngsters), to ensure compliance with rules and specifications. A competitive event may be limited exclusively to one sex; mixed, with both sexes in the same event; or comprised of one of various combinations of youngsters, adults, and senior citizens.

A league is a form of organized competition, with winners usually determined at the end of a nine-month bowling season. League play is most frequently conducted in the evening,

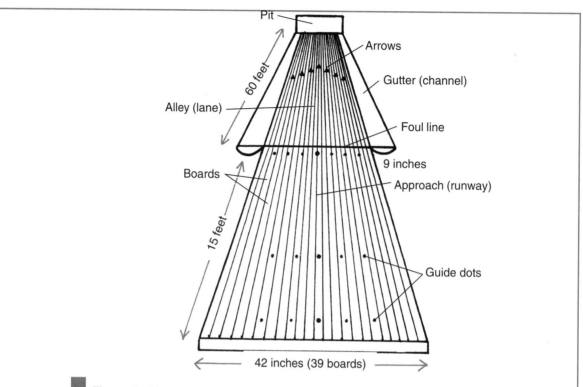

**Figure 4** Dimensions of a bowling lane and its approach.

and monetary prizes are awarded at the end of the league season. Recreational leagues feature small prizes; also, the great diversity of individual bowling skills often necessitates the addition of *handicap* (added pins) to scores. Serious competitive leagues feature larger prizes; there is less diversity of bowling skills, and competition is often conducted as *scratch* (without added handicap).

A tournament is similar to a league, with winners usually determined at the end of a single event. As in leagues, scores may be altered with handicap to encourage greater participation. There may be *medal* play, in which standings are decided by the score; *match* play, in which standings are decided by games or points won; or a combination of both, such as the point system used in PBA tournaments.

## Basic Rules and Scoring

The following is a brief description of playing rules and scoring for the American game of tenpins. For a complete description of current tenpin bowling rules, regulations, and specifications, refer to the current year's edition of the *American Bowling Congress Constitution, Specifications, Rules and Suggested League Rules Manual.*

A game, or game score, of tenpin bowling consists of 10 frames. Each of the first 9 f rames allows two deliveries; the 10th frame allows a third if the player makes a strike or a spare. A *legal delivery* is one in which the ball leaves the player's hand and touches the lane.

*Legal pinfall* may result from a legally delivered ball. Pins may be knocked down by the ball or by other pins rebounding from the *kickboards*, the side walls by the rack of pins; from the *rear cushion* behind the rack; or from the *sweep bar*, the horizontal bar that clears fallen pins off the *pin deck*, the part of the lane where the rack of pins is set (see Figure 5).

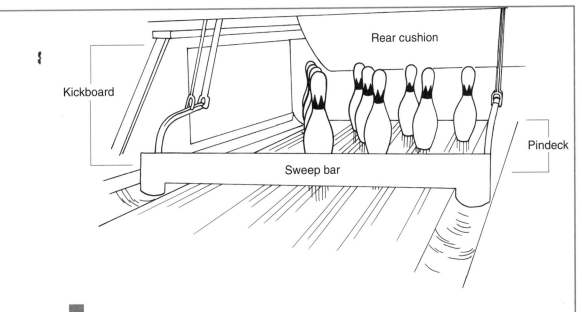

**Figure 5** The bowling lane pin area.

*Illegal pinfall* may also result from a legally delivered ball. Illegal pinfall does not count toward the score and may include pins knocked over by a ball that has left the lane before pin contact, pins knocked over by a ball rebounding from the rear cushion, or pins touched by a pinsetter before they fall. If a *foul* has been committed—some part of the bowler's body having touched the lane or any other portion of the bowling establishment past the foul line—any pinfall is illegal. Pins knocked down by a legal first ball in a frame and remaining on the playing surface are swept off so as not to interfere with a spare attempt at the standing pins.

A bowling score is *cumulative*, that is, pinfall from the current frame is added to that of the previous frames. The maximum score is 300, resulting from bonus pins being given for strikes and spares. (If scoring were simply additive, a maximum score for bowling would probably be between 100 and 240, depending upon whether 10 or 20 points were awarded for a strike and whether there were 10, 11, or 12 deliveries allowed.) To learn how to keep score, see Step 4.

To allow persons of unequal ability to compete with each other, a *handicap* is often added to the *raw*, or *scratch*, score of the bowler with less skill (lower average). Adding handicaps is an attempt to equalize the winning chances of all bowlers in the field.

There are many ways to determine a handicap for a bowler; while none is particularly valid or reliable, there are two popular methods. When handicapping with the *percentage difference* method, you subtract bowler B's score from bowler C's score, and 70, 80, or 90 percent of the difference between the scores of two bowlers (or teams) represents the handicap. With the *percentage from base score* method, you assume some arbitrary *base score*, such as 200, 210, or 220. Each bowler's average score is then subtracted from the base score to get a handicap. For more details on how to determine handicaps, see Step 10.

## Tenpin Bowling Today

The disappearance of smaller neighborhood bowling centers devoted primarily to bowling, and the appearance of large leisure-time complexes in which bowling is only one of the many recreational offerings, have further strengthened bowling's recreational position.

Bowling fulfills the conception of a "sport" held by the recreational bowler because it is a pastime, a form of amusement; the activity, the social interaction, and keeping score are all "fun." Even to the serious bowler or the professional aspirant, bowling can be fun because pursuing excellence is also a form of amusement.

Bowling succeeds as a worthwhile lifetime activity because it provides moderate exercise to persons of all ages. Persons of average strength and agility can compete for prizes and recognition in this sport because it is less demanding than, say, tennis, baseball, or football. Because bowling centers are typically located only a short distance from residential areas, bowling activity is also a convenient way for many persons to have a viable social life. Also, bowling can be an effective way to make friends when traveling or relocating to a new area of the country.

Although mastery of bowling requires great patience and application, it is stimulating for the professional bowler because it provides an opportunity to learn new skills, to talk frequently with persons of similar interests, and to earn the admiration of others. Even practice becomes fun for the serious bowler if it is perceived as such! You will understand this point better after you have progressed through your Steps to Success.

Many options for organized competition are available. Adults may compete in American Bowling Congress and Women's International Bowling Congress leagues and tournaments—sanctioned or unsanctioned. Many short-handicap and scratch-tournament events are conducted in major cities on almost every weekend. Youngsters may compete for fun and recognition in leagues and tournaments sanctioned by the Young American Bowling Alliance, and collegiate bowlers can compete within their collegiate systems. All amateur bowlers may compete for places on the U.S. international teams. Finally, opportunities exist for skilled bowlers to compete for cash prizes in events sanctioned by the Professional Bowlers Association, the Ladies Professional Bowlers Tour, and similar professional organizations.

## Organizations to contact for additional information:

American Bowling Congress (ABC)
5301 S. 76th St.
Greendale, WI 53129

Ladies Professional Bowlers Tour (LPBT)
7171 Cherryvale Blvd.
Rockford, IL 61112

Professional Bowlers Association (PBA)
P.O. Box 5118
1720 Merriman Rd.
Akron, OH 44313

Women's International Bowling Congress (WIBC)
5301 S. 76th St.
Greendale, WI 53129

Young American Bowling Alliance (YABA)
5301 S. 76th St.
Greendale, WI 53129

# Selecting Your Equipment

The word "equipment" in bowling generally refers to what a bowler uses to bowl, that is, the ball and shoes. Occasionally, the term includes the bowling bag. The most important pieces of equipment a bowler can have are a good fitting ball of the proper total weight and a pair of shoes that allow a normal walking pattern to a controlled slide during the release of the ball.

The two features that allow you to maintain an effective grip on the bowling ball are ball *fit* (the size, location, and orientation of the holes in the ball) and the ball's *total weight.* If the ball fit is inappropriate or if the ball is too heavy, you will feel it necessary to squeeze rather than simply hold the ball, creating forearm stress and too tense a grip. Excessive tension in the forearm triggers excessive tension in the upper arm and shoulder joint, destroying the free pendulum swing.

## How the Ball Should Fit

There are three common ball fit styles, also called *grips*, designed to allow gripping the ball with the thumb and portions of the middle and ring fingers. Beginners like the *conventional* grip. Advanced bowlers usually progress to the wider *semifingertip* grip, or to the *fingertip* grip (see Figure 6, a-c). Occasionally you may see a person bowling with the thumb halfway or entirely out of the ball, imparting rapid spin with only the middle and ring fingers. Any technique that does not use the whole thumb to grip the ball, however, does not promote the free-pendulum swing, and is not recommended.

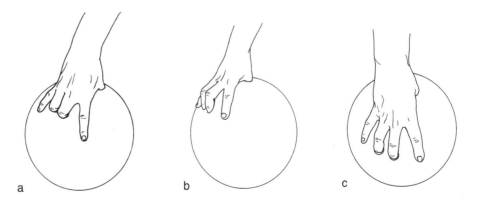

**Figure 6**   (a) Conventional fit, (b) semifingertip fit, (c) and fingertip fit.

The conventional fit allows you to insert your thumb to its base, and your fingers to their second joints. The *span* (the distance between the near edges of the thumbhole and a fingerhole) is proper if the crease of your finger's second joint extends 1/4 inch to 3/8 inch beyond the near edge of its fingerhole, depending on the size of your hand. This fit is the one most commonly found in *house balls* (those provided by the bowling establishment). It is recommended for beginners and persons with weaker hands because it provides a firmer finger hold.

The semifingertip fit allows you to insert your thumb to its base, and your fingers midway between their first and second joints. The span is often judged to be proper if the near edge of the fingerhole contacts your finger anywhere between the creases of its first and second joints. The semifingertip fit does not promote a free-pendulum swing and consequently is not recommended for either beginners or advanced bowlers.

The fingertip fit allows you to insert your thumb to its base and your fingers to their first joints. The span is assumed to be proper if the near edge of the fingerhole lies slightly closer to the tip of your finger than midway between the creases of its first and second joints. This fit places many demands on the bowler and should be used only by advanced bowlers, with fitting done only at qualified pro shops.

## Selecting a House Ball

The bowling establishment provides house balls for bowlers who do not own their own balls. The management of the establishment attempts to keep them arranged in *ball racks* in order of weight, from 6 to 16 pounds. The hole sizes and spans generally increase with increasing total ball weight.

**Note:** If you are a beginner and happen to find either a semifingertip or fingertip grip on a house ball, do not use it.

### Select the Proper Ball Fit

Proper ball fit feels more comfortable, causes less fatigue of the hand and arm, and lessens the chance of injury through pulled muscles, tendinitis, blisters, deep calluses, and so on. To see whether a ball fits your hand, use the following sequence:

1. **Thumbhole Size:** First insert your thumb into the thumbhole. While pressing one side of the thumb lightly to one side of the hole, slide the thumb in and out. If the other side of the thumb barely touches its side, the thumbhole size is appropriate. If the thumbhole is too loose or too tight, try another ball.
2. **Correctness of Span:** After selecting a thumbhole that fits, select a ball with the proper span based on descriptions previously given for the conventional ball.

### Select the Proper Ball Weight

The weight of the ball you use should be appropriate for your physical makeup. You cannot effectively place a ball into your swing if it is too heavy. Further, your hand will not be able to hold the ball as it is falling into the *downswing* (the ball's backward pendular motion before you roll it). The ball will appear to pull your swing shoulder down and back, resulting in a labored, jerky series of movements. On the other hand (figuratively speaking), you will often manhandle a ball that is too light, the weight of the ball being insufficient to signal you to let it swing by its own weight.

Adult male beginner bowlers often choose balls in the 14- to 16-pound range, whereas adult females often choose balls in the 10- to 14-pound range. Youngsters often choose balls ranging from 6 to 14 pounds. Use the following "Holdout Test" and "Trial Swing" sections to check for appropriateness of weight.

1. **Holdout Test**: After selecting the ball on the basis of proper fit, pick it up to test it for total weight. The general rule is to use the heaviest ball that you feel you can control. Hold it directly in front of you with both hands and your elbows locked (see Figure 7). If you cannot hold the ball in this position for at least 5 seconds, it is too heavy; select a lighter ball.
2. **Trial Swing**: Look all around you and give yourself plenty of clearance. If the ball seems to be of an acceptable weight from the holdout test and passes the criteria of proper fit, as explained previously, take a short trial swing. Remember that a ball exerts more downward force at the bottom of the swing, so allow for this centrifugal "weight" when selecting your ball. Be persistent; do not settle for a ball that seems too heavy (see Figure 8).

Ball heaviest here

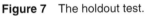 **Figure 7**  The holdout test.  **Figure 8**  The trial swing.

## Problems With House Balls

Most house ball spans are the same for both the middle and the ring fingers, allowing both right- and left-handed bowlers to use house balls with equal opportunity. Unfortunately, the normal hand usually does not require equal spans—a fact that makes most house balls unsuitable for use by more advanced bowlers. The middle-finger span is too wide if the ring-finger span is correct; the ring-finger span is too narrow if the middle-finger span is correct. Also, if the ball is selected on the basis of correct thumb fit, the fingerholes are usually oversized.

Another problem exists with weight imbalances in house balls. There is a heavy spot, *a weight block*, placed in undrilled balls to compensate for the removal of ball material by drilling the holes. Often a substantial amount of this *topweight* is left in the drilled ball. In lighter balls this remaining weight may represent a significant portion of the total weight of the ball. If such a ball is rolled slowly, it may veer off in the direction of the side of the ball in which the topweight is located. A novice bowler using such a ball may be confused and assume that this odd ball reaction resulted from poor technique; this confusion can impede progress.

If you select a ball that exhibits this veering pattern, ask a trained person to assist you in finding another. Fortunately, major manufacturers have recognized this problem and now offer light balls with very little topweight before drilling.

## Selecting a Customized Ball

If you bowl more than a couple of times per month and want to become a better bowler, you must have a better ball fit and good footing. Go to a good *pro shop* to purchase your own ball and shoes. Call around and ask several of the best bowlers in your area for the name of a skillful ball driller. Here are some helpful considerations:

- Try to buy ball, bag, and shoes together if possible, because your shoes are an important element in providing stability for good *leverage* (lift that causes rotation) to be imparted to the ball. Furthermore, a bowler serious enough to own a ball should not have to dole out money continually for rented shoes. The necessity for a bag is also obvious, since other accessories are usually carried in it.
- Do not immerse your hands in water (such as a bath or shower) for at least two hours before you have your ball fitted. If you do, there is a possibility that the grip holes will be fitted too large.
- Exercise your hand before having the ball fitted, to relax your hand, stretching your grip to what it will be after a few practice shots and giving you a better chance for a more accurate span measurement. Otherwise, your span may be fitted too short.
- Tell the pro shop operator if your hands are in frequent contact with slippery or drying solvents or if you have any problems, such as arthritis, that lessen your ability to grip. These factors may necessitate modifications in the fit and the ball weight.
- Tell the pro shop operator what you can afford to spend and where you usually bowl. Such information will have a bearing on the price and type of ball most appropriate for you.

## Selecting a Used Bowling Ball

A used bowling ball can be a good buy because it is cheaper than a new one. There are plenty of used bowling balls available. Many pro shops offer used balls, and members of the PBA and LPBT have good used balls for sale. Teammates often trade balls. All these are sources of better quality used balls. Pawn shops and garage sales often sell used balls, too, but be cautious—many balls found in these places prove to be damaged, due to improper storage.

If you are considering buying a used ball, check the cover for deep cracks or abrasions. Check to see whether the cover of the ball is solidly bonded to the core. If the ball has a badly damaged cover or if the ball sounds nonuniform or hollow when you tap it with a blunt object, pass it up. If you do find an acceptable used ball, take it to a pro shop for the appropriate fit. In most cases, the driller will have to *plug* and redrill all of the holes with your own customized grip.

## Gripping Aids

Often your hands may be too wet or too dry to grip the ball effectively. Just as in other sports, there are various gripping aids in bowling. One is a small, porous bag containing rosin powder, which can help you attain a better grip. Another is a rosin cream. Both the powder and the cream build up on your hands and should be washed off or removed with rubbing alcohol. These substances also build up in the holes of your ball, so you are advised to use them sparingly and only if absolutely necessary.

You may have *finger inserts* installed in your customized ball. These gripping aids, made of plastic, help you grip your ball and impart more lift with your fingers at the release with less effort. These grips also reduce the size of the holes. Cork or rubber gripping pads are available, with adhesive backing for sticking inside the holes on the gripping surfaces.

Another way to adjust the size of a gripping hole is to place several layers of smooth plastic tape in the back side of the hole, opposite the gripping surface. Unlike using cork and rubber grips, this method will take up space without increasing friction.

## Selecting Shoes

In all sports, a stable *base of support* for your body is vital. Tennis players are taught to stay low and stretch out, golfers dig in when addressing the ball, and baseball players must keep their knees flexed so that they can make turns quickly. All of these actions require good footing, so special shoes are used to enhance stability through greater traction. Bowling shoes are designed to give you a stable base of support to maintain balance during your approach and to promote good leverage during the release.

### *House Rental Shoes*

Ask the control counter supervisor for house shoes one-half size smaller than your street shoes. If you are obtaining shoes for someone else, be sure to designate whether they are for a man or a woman, because shoes of similar numerical designation differ in size between the sexes. Remember to return your house shoes to the control counter when you are finished bowling.

### *Personal Commercial Bowling Shoes*

In order to accommodate both right- and left-handed bowlers, house shoes have leather on both soles (see Figure 9, a and b). This compromise does not promote good bowling form and results in less stability in the delivery. Therefore, it is recommended that you purchase your own bowling shoes.

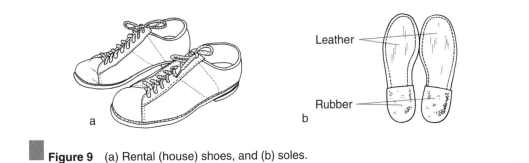

Leather

Rubber

a          b

**Figure 9**   (a) Rental (house) shoes, and (b) soles.

Good quality commercial bowling shoes allow a skid-free and stick-free heel-toe walk to the foul line; a stable anchoring of your *propelling* (nonsliding, or pushing) foot (erroneously called the *braking foot)* in preparation for the slide; and a smooth, continuous sliding motion of the *sliding* foot toward the foul line.

Make sure that your bowling shoes fit properly. Naturally, you will not buy shoes that are too short or narrow, but also avoid shoes that are too large. Such shoes allow your foot to slide inside, causing instability. A padded arch can be helpful in preventing unnecessary internal movement. The lace-to-toe models can be adjusted to accommodate the width of the foot, so this style is recommended.

Your shoes should not tire your feet. The soles should be rather thick, keeping the ball of your foot from flexing too much. If possible, the shoe should have a steel shank to keep your arch from stretching too much.

Your sliding sole should allow a free slide; it should be made of leather. In addition, your pushing sole (on your propelling foot) should supply sufficient traction to allow you to push your body forward into your slide. Buy only bowling shoes with a leather sliding sole and a rubber propelling sole (see Figure 10, a and b).

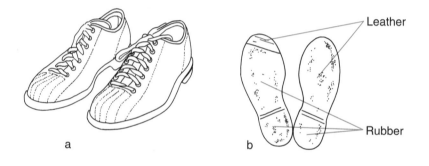

Leather

Rubber

a          b

**Figure 10**   (a) Right-handed commercial bowling shoes, and (b) soles.

Avoid the *universal sole* models in which the soles of both shoes are made of the same composite material. Both heels should be made of rubber to prevent slippage as your weight moves from the heel to the toe during walking.

### Personal Custom-Made Bowling Shoes

If your feet are difficult to fit with commercial bowling shoes, you can purchase custom-made shoes. Your feet must be measured for these shoes, so you may want to locate a pro shop that will measure your feet and place the order for you. Otherwise, you may take the measurements yourself, using forms supplied by a shoe company.

## Choosing a Bowling Bag

You need a sturdy bag in which to carry your ball and shoes. It must be spacious enough for additional items, such as a shirt, a towel, an accessory bag, and various hand and wrist supports. You can use many different types of bags, but a bag's true tests are how well it protects your bowling ball and shoes from damage and how easy it is to carry to and from the bowling center.

Purchase the bag that is appropriate for you with respect to cost, image, and utility. If you are rough on your equipment, a molded, hardcover type may be best for you. If you bowl only occasionally and are very fastidious with your equipment, a vinyl or Naugahyde bag may be acceptable. If you bowl many tournaments, you may prefer a canvas bag, the kind easiest to carry and store under the settee.

*Consumer tip:* Most bags manufactured for the purpose of carrying bowling balls are sufficiently sturdy. Other bags that resemble them may not be, so beware! It is recommended that you choose a bag that has (a) heavy or double stitching; (b) strong clasps; and (c) shoulder or handle straps that extend all the way around the bag, overlap, and are stitched to themselves.

## Wrist Supports

A *technique-supportive* wrist support promotes proper form by allowing greater rotation and a quicker thumb release. All supports keep the wrist immobile during the delivery. Some supports hold the wrist straight *(extended)*; some direct the hand in toward the front of the forearm *(cupped)*; some direct the hand up toward the back of the forearm *(back-extended)*; and some are adjustable to accomplish all three objectives (see Figure 11, a-c).

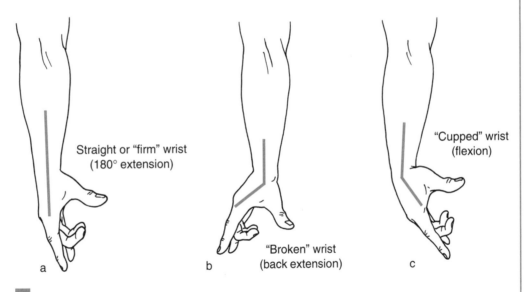

**Figure 11**   Various wrist positions.

Remember, wrist supports may also hinder proper form, being *technique-interfering.* They may hold your wrist in an uncomfortable position, or they may make you drop your ball before you are ready to release it. If such problems exist for you, consult a qualified pro shop operator for assistance.

## The Accessory Bag

In addition to your ball, shoes, and towel, you may want to carry these other useful items in an accessory bag inside your bowling bag.

- Adhesive tape: cloth tape used to increase traction on the gripping surface inside a gripping hole
- Plastic tape: used in the back of a gripping hole to reduce its size
- Scotch Brite: nylon webbing used to clean shoe soles and heels

- New Skin: used to cover abrasions on the fingers and thumb
- Extra shoelaces
- Adhesive bandages

The contents of your accessory bag will change over the years as lane conditions evolve, as the frequency of your bowling changes, and as new products appear on the market.

## Clothing

In order to ensure freedom of movement during the bowling delivery, you must be careful in your choice of clothing for bowling.

*Slacks:* If you are short-waisted, avoid long-waisted slacks; these will slide down, inhibiting movement of your upper legs. If your pants legs are too tight, you will not be able to bend your knees as deeply as necessary for good shotmaking, a shortcoming which becomes most apparent in your last step and slide. Also avoid blue jeans (which feature tight legs and heavy, irritating inseams) and shorts (they ride up, and the bottoms bind your legs at midthigh).

*Shirt or Blouse:* Avoid shirts and blouses with a continuous seam up the side and into the sleeve. Try to wear knit shirts or blouses that allow free range of motion for your swing. Raglan sleeves are also desirable. A tight shirt keeps your shoulders from being held high and back (the preferred orientation). Also avoid sweaters (too bulky; they make your swing move away from your body) and long-sleeved shirts (which bind your elbows). Do not tuck your shirt or blouse too tightly into your slacks or skirt.

*Especially for Women:* If possible avoid wearing panty hose—especially tight hose that keep you from bending your legs sufficiently during your last step and slide. The added tension at the knee gives you a silent signal to keep your legs too straight. Also avoid full skirts (which make your swing move away from your body) and tight skirts (which bind your thighs).

*Distracting Items:* Other items sufficiently distracting to interfere with proper technique are key chains, scabbards, and electronic pagers attached to the belt; towels in the pockets; hats, caps, and unrestrained long hair; and loose eyeglasses.

## Preparing Your Body for Success

Before you bowl, you need to warm up with moderate toning and limbering exercises. Perform your warm-up within five minutes of bowling so that its effects are not lost. Your warm-up starts when you walk into the building and get yourself ready to bowl. It is important to stretch a warm muscle. Gently hold stretches 6 to 8 seconds without bouncing; just lean into the stretch gradually. Areas to loosen up include your shoulders, arms, hands, lower back, upper thighs, and ankles.

Usually, only strenuous sports have a cool-down. However, make time for some short cool-down exercises to relieve your hands, feet, hips, lower back, and legs after extended bowling activity. A cool-down routine restores flexibility and promotes circulation.

# STEP 1

## SETUP: GAINING POSITION AND BALANCE

Generally speaking, archers, pistol shooters, and golfers take more care in setting themselves up than bowlers. Watch the next pro golf tournament and see how players like Jack Nicklaus and Greg Norman set up before each swing. A good golfer aligns the body perfectly in order to direct the ball to its target—before the swing starts. You, and other bowlers, should do the same each attempt, every frame.

The preparation for movement in the bowling delivery is often called the *stance* or the *address,* but the word *setup* has more meaning because it tells you that you should systematically set yourself up in preparation for consistent, accurate movement.

## Why Is the Setup Important?

The better the setup, the better the delivery, so it is important that you make the same complete series of checks, starting with your feet and moving upward, *every* time you step onto the approach. If you were attempting to roll a hoop across a gymnasium floor at a selected target, you would not carelessly nudge the hoop to send it on its way. You would first make sure that the hoop was perfectly in line with its intended path and perpendicular to the floor. In doing so, you would be keeping the hoop's *center of gravity* (the balance point—the place where the hoop's weight is centered) under control and give it a better chance to go straighter.

Good balance and accuracy, the benefits of maintaining control of your own center of gravity during movement, begin with a well-balanced setup. If you systematically set yourself up in proper balance—with your feet supporting your hips, your shoulders parallel with your hips, your back muscles stable, and your ball in line with your shoulder and the intended target—you will be better prepared to keep

your center of gravity from swinging side to side during your delivery.

## How to Execute the Setup

To begin, carefully pick up your ball by its sides off the ball return. Place it in your nonbowling or *balance* hand, to avoid unnecessary tension in your bowling arm. Stand about 2 feet from the end of the approach, near the center, and look at the set of dots closest to you (see Figure 1.1a). This is termed the *next-up position.*

From the next-up position, check for clearance of bowlers to either side of you and step up onto the approach to begin your setup ritual. Because you need a specific place to stand and to look at while you are setting up, place the inner edge of the sole of your sliding foot on the dot 5 boards to the *outside* (to your *swingside,* the side of the lane nearer your bowling arm) of the large center dot of either set of approach dots (see Figure 1.1b).

Next, bring your feet together so that your toes and heels form a square and that the inner edges of both feet are 2 to 3 inches apart and pointed straight toward your target (second arrow on your swingside). Be sure that your knees are straight, your hips and shoulders parallel with each other and perpendicular to your feet. You are "squaring" or "squaring up" (see Figure 1.1c). Hold your back upright and your head high—be "snooty"!

Next, put your fingers into the gripping holes first, then your thumb (review Figure 6), and transfer your ball to a position in line with your bowling arm and the second arrow. Do not bend your thumb. If necessary, move your feet, turning your entire body so your shoulders are 90 degrees to this shoulder-ball-target "gun." Maintain the parallel relationship between your hips and shoulders. Keep your forearm slightly raised up and hold most of the ball's weight in your balance arm, not your bowling arm. Stare at the second arrow from the swingside channel, slowly take a deep breath, slowly exhale, and hold your stomach in (see Figure 1.1d).

FIGURE
1.1

**KEYS TO SUCCESS**

# SETUP (right-handed bowler)

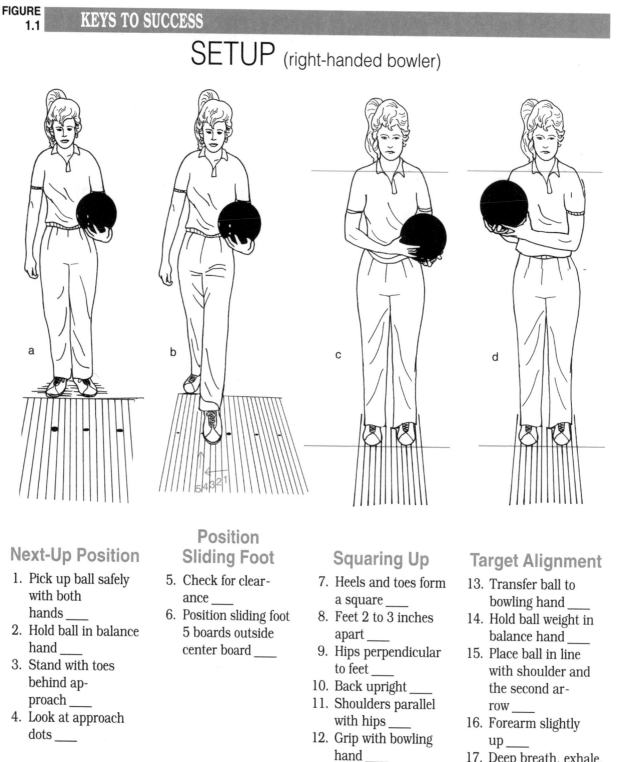

a   b   c   d

### Next-Up Position
1. Pick up ball safely with both hands ___
2. Hold ball in balance hand ___
3. Stand with toes behind approach ___
4. Look at approach dots ___

### Position Sliding Foot
5. Check for clearance ___
6. Position sliding foot 5 boards outside center board ___

### Squaring Up
7. Heels and toes form a square ___
8. Feet 2 to 3 inches apart ___
9. Hips perpendicular to feet ___
10. Back upright ___
11. Shoulders parallel with hips ___
12. Grip with bowling hand ___

### Target Alignment
13. Transfer ball to bowling hand ___
14. Hold ball weight in balance hand ___
15. Place ball in line with shoulder and the second arrow ___
16. Forearm slightly up ___
17. Deep breath, exhale, and stomach in ___
18. Remain steady ___

## SETUP SUCCESS STOPPERS

You'll make more accurate *shots* (deliveries) if you correct setup errors before beginning movement. Although some errors may be obvious, you may not realize the effects of other errors until you have begun your approach or even released the ball.

| Error | Correction |
|---|---|
| 1. Your sliding foot is not at its proper setup location. | 1. Place the inner edge of your sliding foot on the first dot to the outside of the large center dot. |
| 2. Your swingside foot is not even with your sliding foot. | 2. Position your feet so that your toes and heels form a square. |
| 3. One or both knees are bent. | 3. Straighten your knees just short of the locked position. |
| 4. You hold your ball too low. | 4. Hold your ball with your wrist slightly higher than your elbow. |
| 5. You hold your ball either too close to the center of your body or too far away from it. | 5. Put your ball in line with your shoulder and the target. |
| 6. Too much of the ball's weight is on your bowling arm. | 6. Place your balance hand under your bowling hand and lift with your balance hand. |
| 7. Your head or your shoulders are too far forward. | 7. Keep your head up. Be "snooty" and look out of the bottoms of your eyes. |

**SETUP**

# DRILLS

## *1. Check Sequence Run-Through*

How well do you know your setup check sequence? The better you know it, the faster you can execute the setup correctly. Study the Setup Keys to Success in Figure 1.1 thoroughly. When ready, take your ball and act out each item as you recite it aloud. At the end of the sequence, check, and compute your score. You may use a partner to help you.

**Success Goal** = Recite and perform all 18 Keys to Success in 5 or fewer attempts ___

**Success Check**
• Pick up ball safely ___
• Step onto approach ___
• Act out setup Keys to Success ___

**To Increase Difficulty**
• Execute from memory with no partner prompting, creating your own memory aid, such as a poem or a rhythmic chant.

**To Decrease Difficulty**
• Use no ball or a lighter ball.
• Have a partner read each Key aloud to you as you execute each one.
• Select only one group of items at a time, then move on to the next group when ready, adding to the previous group.

## *2. Balance Awareness*

Can you feel when you are in balance or off balance? From your correct setup position, lean forward slowly, paying close attention to the shifting of your weight to the balls of your feet. Lean forward just enough to feel that you are about to lose your balance. Return to the upright position. Next lean to the swingside, paying attention to weight distribution on the feet. Lean to the swingside just enough to feel your balance-side foot lift off of the approach.

**Success Goal =**
a. 5 comparisons of forward leans, and of balance ___
b. 5 comparisons of swingside leans, and of balance ___

**Success Check**
• Set up correctly ___
• Compare in-balance with off-balance awareness ___
• Concentrate on feeling of balance ___

**To Increase Difficulty**
• Close your eyes after assuming the completed setup position and repeat the drill.

**To Decrease Difficulty**
• Use a lighter ball.
• Do only the number of comparisons necessary to give you a clear idea of being off balance.
• Accomplish the drill with a partner facing you, doing each comparison with you at the same time.

### 3. Alignment Awareness

Can you feel how well your shoulder and ball are aligned with the second arrow? From the completed setup position, while keeping your eyes on the second arrow, look at your swingside shoulder, then at the ball, and finally at the second arrow. Move so that the three lie along an imaginary straight line perfectly perpendicular to your shoulders.

a. Now, reposition your feet so that your toes are pointed 3 inches to the outside. Keep your body segments in the same relationship as before. Note that your shoulder, the ball, and the second arrow are no longer aligned. Reposition the ball so that it is aligned with the second arrow and note that you are holding your ball too far to the inside. Return to your correctly aligned position.

b. Next, reposition your feet so that your toes are pointed 3 inches to the inside. Keep your body segments in the same relationship as before. Note that your shoulder, the ball, and the second arrow are no longer aligned. Reposition the ball so that it is aligned with the second arrow and note that you are holding your ball too far to the outside. Return to your correctly aligned position.

#### Success Goal =

a. 5 comparisons of inside misalignments with correct alignments ___

b. 5 comparisons of outside misalignments with correct alignments ___

#### Success Check

- Stand in normal setup ___
- Align bowling shoulder and ball correctly with second arrow ___
- Misalign ball to inside and compare with correct alignment ___
- Misalign ball to outside and compare with correct alignment ___
- Support ball's weight in your balance hand and arm ___

#### To Increase Difficulty

- Become aware of unnecessary tension in your bowling hand, forearm, and upper arm and try to willfully reduce this tension while your body is correctly aligned.

#### To Decrease Difficulty

- Use a lighter-weight ball.
- Do only the number of comparisons necessary to give you a clear idea of being misaligned.
- Ask a partner to tape one end of a length of string to your shoulder and to hold the other end on the second arrow; use this device as an aid to alignment.

## SETUP SUCCESS SUMMARY

Be sure that your setup is stable, well balanced, and accurately aligned with your target. Ask your teacher, coach, or practice partner to evaluate your technique according to the Keys to Success checklist items within Figure 1.1.

# STEP

## 2

# SWING AND CADENCE: ADDING A CONSISTENT RHYTHM

S ome of the greatest bowlers in the history of bowling are Billy Welu, Dick Weber, and Earl Anthony. The unhurried consistency of their swings is beautiful to watch; the results are even more beautiful.

Just like the pendulum on a grandfather clock, your bowling arm must be a free pendulum during the delivery. You should use no muscular force to speed up or slow down the ball. Your ball must simply fall into the downswing, then back to the top of the backswing, then down, into the forward swing, drawn only by the force of gravity.

To achieve a consistent swing, it is vital that you integrate the movement of your upper body into a smooth, rhythmic sequence, and that the feel of this coordinated movement is ingrained. By integrating three basic skills—the pushaway and the takeaway (position of your balance arm) with your particular pendulum swing's timing—you'll avoid making execution errors that can lower your bowling scores. Both the takeaway and the pendulum swing begin the instant that the pushaway ends. Whether a part-

ner assists you in a modified setup position, or you start from your setup position during the drills in this step, you'll learn the feel of the ideal free-pendulum swing and the feel of undesirable deviations from this ideal.

## Why Is the Pendulum Swing Important?

A musician uses a metronome to establish a consistent rhythm, or *cadence*, for a musical performance. You can use the all-important free-pendulum swing to establish a consistent cadence. If you always allow your ball to swing as an unforced or uninhibited pendulum from the same position, you will have one consistent timing element around which to build your entire approach and delivery when you add your footwork. Figure 2.1 shows the timing for the pendulum swing from its stationary shoulder position.

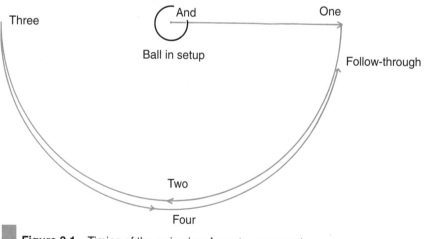

**Figure 2.1** Timing of the swing in a four-step approach.

## How to Execute the Pushaway

A properly executed pushaway promotes (1) a free-pendulum swing, with more natural (unforced) ball speed; and (2) accuracy, by keeping the swing plane in line with your intended visual fixation point, or visual target. The proper technique for the pushaway is the act of pushing the ball with both hands into the desired plane of the swing at the predetermined height, in line with the swing shoulder and a desired visual fixation point.

Seeing where your ball is at the *end* of your pushaway is as important as attaining the feel of a proper pushaway. You need to push away the ball accurately in line with a target. A ball placed reasonably high into the swing represents more potential energy than a ball placed lower. The lower your pushaway, the lower your backswing (if you do not hoist, or pull the ball up into the backswing) and the shorter the total swing time. The higher your pushaway, the higher your backswing (if you do not clip, or stop the backswing before it reaches the top of the backswing) and the longer your total swing time.

A well-executed pushaway promotes accuracy by keeping the swing plane in line with your intended visual fixation point, or visual target. A misaligned swing tends to pull you off balance; more effort is needed to maintain control of your center of gravity. If you direct your pushaway too close to the front center of your body, you have to counteract this imbalance with a step to the outside (when you add footwork to your swing). If your pushaway is directed too far to the outside, you have to compensate by stepping to the inside (when you add footwork to your swing).

Start in your setup position. Mentally count your cadence, "and, one, two, three, four." On the "and" start your pushaway. Be sure to support the ball firmly with your balance hand during the pushaway. Prepare to move on an "and" count. Be in your extended setup position on the count of "one" (see Figure 2.2). To prevent injury to your elbow keep it straight (or locked) as the ball drops into the swing. Otherwise, your bent elbow will be snapped into the straight position by the weight of the ball.

The locking of both elbows should not involve any violent thrusting of the ball into the straight-out position. Locking is a low-stress stabilization of completely extended arms after a decisive, continuous movement of the ball from the setup position to the final pushaway destination. Your ball should be straight out in front of your bowling shoulder with your shoulders forming a 90-degree angle on the count of "one" (see Figure 2.3).

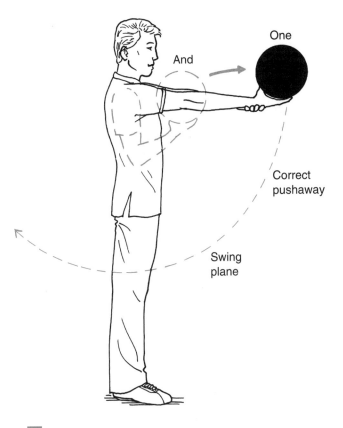

**Figure 2.2** Pushaway timing to extended arm position.

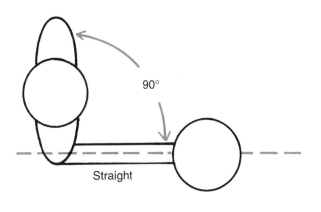

**Figure 2.3** Overhead view of shoulders perpendicular to the swing arm.

## How to Execute the Takeaway

The takeaway is the movement of the balance arm from a position of supporting the ball in the fully extended pushaway to a position out from the body, slightly down, and slightly toward the back. The balance arm is held in this position throughout the delivery.

When the balance arm is taken away in synchrony with the fall of the ball into the swing and is held in the proper position, it counterbalances some of the weight of the ball. More importantly, the balance arm stabilizes the pivot for the swing. Thus, an imaginary line—running from the swing shoulder through the other shoulder to the balance hand—may be pictured as an axis around which the swing rotates (see Figure 2.4). In keeping your swing shoulder from dropping too low and both shoulders from rotating, your balance arm—if carefully timed, placed, and held in the proper position—helps to ensure against misdirected shots. Otherwise, rotating shoulders allow your swing to deviate from the ideal swing plane, causing a *bumpout*, a *wraparound*, or a combination of both (called a *looped swing*).

## How to Execute the Pendulum Swing

From your extended pushaway position, you simply allow gravity to draw the ball down, up, and back; you neither pull it down nor keep it from falling. Your elbow should be extended *before the ball drops*, your wrist should be straight and firm, and your shoulder should act as a *pivot* or centerpoint for the swing.

Identify your specific cadence as follows: From your setup position, prepare to move on the "and," and push away to extend both arms by count "one" (see Figures 2.1 and 2.5a). Then, let gravity start the ball's pendulum swing. Mentally count "two" as the ball passes your swingside leg. On "three" the ball should reach the top of your backswing. Lastly, on "four" your ball should be passing your swingside leg during the forward swing (see Figure 2.5b). Let the momentum continue until the ball gets shoulder level, then let the ball come back into your two-handed setup position (see Figure 2.5c).

**Figure 2.4** The takeaway, or balance arm, stabilizes the pivot for the swing.

**FIGURE 2.5**

## KEYS TO SUCCESS

# COORDINATED PUSHAWAY, TAKEAWAY, AND PENDULUM SWING

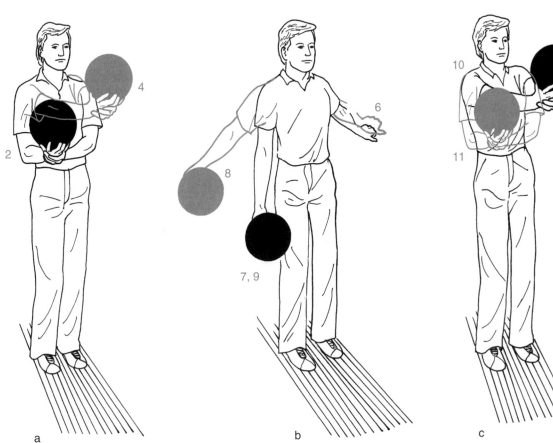

a                b                c

### Preparation

1. Setup position ___
2. Prepare to move on count "and" ___
3. Push away ___
4. Both arms extend (elbows locked) on count "one" ___

### Execution

5. After count "one," let ball fall ___
6. Balance-arm in proper takeaway position ___
7. Count "two," ball by swingside leg ___
8. Count "three," ball at top of backswing ___
9. Count "four," ball by swingside leg ___

### Recovery

10. Keep shoulders, torso, and hips square ___
11. Come back to setup position ___

## SWING AND CADENCE SUCCESS STOPPERS

You can markedly increase your accuracy if you learn how to recognize errors in the coordination of three skills: the pushaway, the takeaway, and the free-pendulum swing. Unless the pushaway is carefully positioned into the swing plane, errors may occur in the direction of the ball when it goes down the lane. Seemingly small errors in the pushaway can result in large errors by the time the ball reaches the point of impact with the pins.

A properly directed free-pendulum swing and takeaway appear to be relatively effortless. However, to the untrained eye, even a retarded, hurried, or misaligned swing may appear to be correct; of course, such characteristics are undesirable. You can increase your consistency through a properly aligned free-pendulum swing if you learn how to recognize the differences between the correct and incorrect pendulum swing characteristics and know how to correct them. Some common pushaway, takeaway, and pendulum swing errors and suggestions on how to correct them follow.

| Error | Correction |
| --- | --- |
| **Pushaway** | |
| 1. You push the ball away either too high or too low. | 1. Push the ball no higher than your shoulders. Aim the ball toward a level 2 to 3 inches higher than the level the ball was in your setup position. |
| 2. You push the ball away either too far to the inside or too far to the outside of the swing. | 2. Push the ball away in line with your shoulder and your target (second arrow). |
| 3. You round off the pushaway. | 3. Be sure to support the ball firmly with your balance hand during the pushaway. Keep your shoulders back. Let your elbows straighten (lock) before letting gravity take the ball's weight into the swing plane. |
| **Takeaway** | |
| 1. You take your balance hand away either too early or too late. | 1. Wait until the end of count "one" to begin your takeaway—just as your ball begins its fall into the swing. |
| 2. Your balance arm moves to the wrong position during the takeaway. | 2. After the count of "one," say to yourself, "Point to the wall," then crisply move your balance arm to the out, down, and back position. |
| **Pendulum Swing** | |
| 1. Your swing arm is not perpendicular to your shoulders. | 1. Square your shoulders to your feet and align your bowling hand with your shoulder. |
| 2. Your elbow is bent. | 2. Keep your shoulders stable and lock your elbows. |
| 3. Your wrist is too loose and hyperextended. | 3. Contract the muscles of your forearm and lift your palm toward your shoulder to give a straighter wrist. |

## SWING AND CADENCE

# DRILLS

*Safety Tips*: Some of the following drills position you face-to-face with a partner. Your partner may be receiving the ball or starting and stopping your swing. Be careful! Always keep your eyes open and look in the direction of your partner. While standing on the approach, swing only in line with the approach and never at an angle to it. Always check behind you before swinging a ball. Warn your partner to keep face and hands clear of your swing.

### *1. Pushaway Placement and Coordination*

Have your partner stand on the approach, face-to-face with you and approximately 3 feet away. Your partner should be ready for you to place your ball into his or her hands at the proper time in your pushaway. Your partner's hands, held 2 to 3 inches higher than your ball in the setup position, represent your *pushaway destination*.

You should begin counting the cadence aloud. On the "and," be ready to push the ball with both hands, with the weight carried by the balance hand (see Figure a), so that it arrives into your partner's waiting hands on "one" (see Figure b). Be gentle when you push your ball into your partner's hands! Do not close your eyes and do not take any steps!

a. Push on "and"

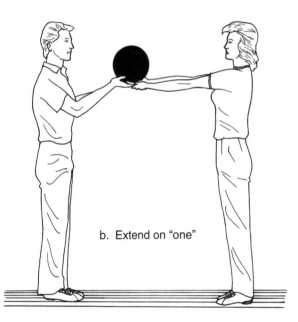

b. Extend on "one"

**Success Goal** = 20 correctly timed pushaways to partner ___

✔ **Success Check**
• Use your balance hand to carry the ball's weight ___
• Fully extend elbows ___
• Keep back and shoulder stable ___

**To Increase Difficulty**
• Take a normal setup, but use your balance hand to grip the ball (to build strength).

**To Decrease Difficulty**
• Use no ball or a lighter ball.

## 2. High and Low Pushaway Awareness

This drill and the following one illustrate common pushaway errors so that you can correct such errors when they occur. Set up for each of the following exercises exactly as you did with the previous drill, with your partner assisting you. Now, however, deliberately change your pushaway destination to an incorrect one so you can study how the error looks and feels. In each case, ask yourself whether you feel strained, stooped, or less stable.

a. *Feeling an excessively high pushaway.* Have your partner hold waiting hands 1 to 2 feet higher than in the previous drill. On the "and" count, begin to push the ball away to this higher destination at count "one."

b. *Feeling an excessively low pushaway.* Have your partner hold waiting hands 1 to 2 feet lower than in the previous drill. On the "and" count, begin to push the ball away to this lower destination at count "one."

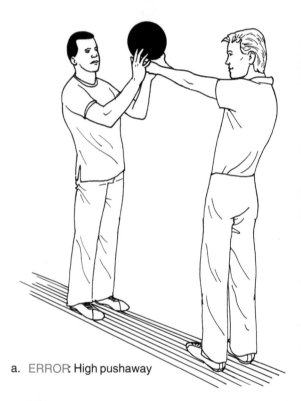

a. ERROR: High pushaway

b. ERROR: Low pushaway

### Success Goal =

a. Compare 5 high with 5 correct pushaways __

b. Compare 5 low with 5 correct pushaways __

### Success Check

- Recognize high/low pushaway errors __
- Recognize correct pushaway destination __
- Fully extend arms on count "one" __

### To Increase Difficulty

- Alternately compare one error with one correct pushaway.
- Randomly call out the pushaway destination prior to executing it.

### To Decrease Difficulty

- Compare one error with one correction at a time, using as many repetitions as necessary to feel the differences.

### 3. Inside and Outside Pushaway Awareness

One of the most persistent and unnoticed errors is that of pushing the ball away to the inside or the outside of the intended swing plane. Small deviations from the ideal here can mean missing the desired point of pin impact by a large margin.

    a. *Inside (convergent) pushaway.* Have your partner hold waiting hands 6 to 8 inches farther to the inside than in the first drill. At the proper time, push the ball away to this more inside destination (see Figure a). Note the feeling of being cramped, with the ball moving somewhat across your body, and the feeling of being out of balance.

    b. *Outside (divergent) pushaway.* Have your partner hold waiting hands 6 to 8 inches farther to the outside than the ideal pushaway. At the proper time, push the ball away to this more outside destination (see Figure b). Note the feeling of being loose or off balance to the outside, with the ball moving somewhat away from your body.

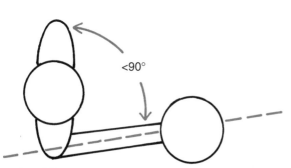

a. ERROR: Convergent pushaway

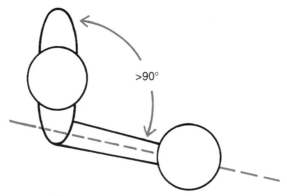

b. ERROR: Divergent pushaway

**Success Goal** =

    a. Compare 5 inside with 5 correct pushaways ___

    b. Compare 5 outside with 5 correct pushaways ___

**Success Check**

- Less than 90-degree angle between shoulders and swing arm (inside error) ___
- Greater than 90-degree angle between shoulders and swing arm (outside error) ___
- Squared or 90-degree angle between shoulders with swing arm (correct pushaway) ___

**To Increase Difficulty**

- Alternately compare one error with one correct pushaway.
- Randomly call out the pushaway destination prior to executing it.

**To Decrease Difficulty**

- Compare one error with one correction at a time, using as many repetitions as necessary to feel the differences.

## 4. Free-Pendulum Swing

Learn how a free-pendulum swing should feel! Hold the ball in an extension setup position (see Figure a). Let your partner hold the weight of the ball by placing the palms of his or her hands on either side of the ball. Your partner should prepare you by saying, "Let me have all of the weight of your ball . . . more . . . more." When he or she feels that you have given up most of the weight of the ball and if you are squared to him or her, with your elbow locked and your wrist firm, your partner should say, "When you are ready, close your eyes and say *one*." Brace yourself by holding your back upright in preparation for the ball to fall. When you feel ready to allow the ball to swing, say "one." Upon hearing your signal, your partner will let the ball fall into the swing (see Figure b).

(*Note*: If you tend to lose your grip on the ball as it starts into the downswing, it may be improperly fitted, too heavy, or both. In this case, have your ball checked by a trained person, and replace it if necessary.)

Simply follow the ball's arc with your arm. Do not allow your upper body to move! Focus on the stability of your body and your shoulder joint. Do not retard or accelerate the swing (see Figure c). Either is termed *muscling the ball,* and must be avoided, or the consistency of the total swing time will disappear.

When the ball passes your swingside leg, your partner should say "two"; when the ball reaches the top of your backswing, your partner should say "three"; and when the ball again passes the swingside leg on the forward swing, your partner should say "four." Then, extend your balance hand to re-grasp the ball's weight and bring the ball into your setup position again. Your partner's count indicates the cadence established by your swing, so remember it well!

a. Extend ball and arms

b. Let ball fall

Count 3

Count 2

Count 4

c. Free swing

**Success Goal** = 10 consecutive free-pendulum swings ___

**Success Check**
- Ball in partner's hands on "one" ___
- Let ball fall into swing ___
- Note speed of swing cadence ___
- Be careful! ___

**To Increase Difficulty**
- Close your eyes to focus on the feel of your swing.
- Either verbally or mentally call out your swing's cadence.
- Start in a setup position, push away into a free-pendulum swing, and come back to a setup position.

**To Decrease Difficulty**
- Use a lighter-weight ball.
- When returning to an extended pushaway position, ask your partner to stop the ball with his or her hands on the sides of the ball.

## 5. Pushaway and Swing Coordination

As necessary, review Figure 2.5, then start from a setup position on the approach. Mentally count your cadence, "and, one, two, three, four." On the "and" start your pushaway. On the "one," your arms should be in an extended position straight from your bowling shoulder. Let gravity take over. Count "two" as the ball passes your swingside leg. Count "three" as the ball reaches the top of your backswing. Count "four" as the ball again passes your swingside leg. Let the ball's momentum continue until shoulder level, then bring the ball back to your two-handed setup position.

**Success Goal** = To identify and competently demonstrate your swing's cadence ___

**Success Check**
- Prepare to move on "and" ___
- Extend both arms on "one" ___
- Ball passes swingside leg on "two" ___
- Ball at top of backswing on "three" ___
- Ball passes swingside leg on "four" ___
- Resume two-handed setup position ___

**To Increase Difficulty**
- Close your eyes to feel the timing of your swing. Then, mentally rehearse your cadence before executing it again.

**To Decrease Difficulty**
- Ask a partner to call out your swing's cadence so you can hear the rhythm.

## 6. Muscling Awareness

Muscling, which is extremely difficult to feel, will cause the timing of your swing to become erratic and make your delivery inconsistent. There are two ways of muscling the ball—retarding (or slowing it down) and accelerating (or speeding it up). Muscling is not difficult to stop if you study it carefully and replace muscling by willfully letting your arm and ball swing freely at the shoulder. Do the following exercises from a partner-assisted extension position. Return to your two-handed setup position at the end.

a. *Feeling a retarded swing.* Just before telling your partner that you are ready, deliberately tense your arm by lifting a little of the weight of the ball slightly up while it is still in your partner's hands. Let your partner know what you are doing. Then close your eyes and say "one," whereupon your partner releases the ball. Keep your arm in this slightly tense state during the entire swing. Focus your attention on the tension in your arm and notice that your swing seems slower than the free swing.

b. *Feeling an accelerated swing.* Just before signaling your partner that you are ready, deliberately pull the ball down slightly while it is still in your partner's hands. Let your partner know what you are doing. Then close your eyes and say "one." Keep your arm in this tense state during the swing. Focus your attention on the tension in your arm and notice that the swing seems faster than the free swing.

Note the speed of the swing while your partner counts "two, three, four," as the ball passes the positions indicated in the above drill. Pull down a little more each time, adding to the ball's weight in your partner's hands before you start your swing.

### Success Goal =

a. Compare 3 retarded swing speeds (slow, slower, slowest) with a free-pendulum swing ___

b. Compare 3 accelerated swing speeds (fast, faster, fastest) with a free-pendulum swing ___

### Success Check

• Swing ball with deliberate muscling ___
• Retard swing speed by lifting the weight up ___
• Accelerate swing speed by pulling the weight down ___
• Let gravity pull the ball through its swing path ___

### To Increase Difficulty

• Do this drill without a partner by holding your ball in front of you as directed in the Holdout Test (review Figure 7).
• Do this drill without a partner, starting and ending in your setup position.

### To Decrease Difficulty

• Use a lighter-weight ball.

### 7. Hoist and Clip Awareness

In this drill you'll practice two errors so that you can feel the difference between them, recognize any tendency to make these errors, and correct them. Neither error is as distinct from a regular setup or an extension setup as it will be when you take a full approach.

a. *Feeling a hoist.* A hoist is the act of pulling the ball up into the backswing with the muscles of the back of the arm, the shoulder, and the back; it is not a free swing. Common causes of the hoist are a low or late pushaway, or leaning over as the ball begins to go down into the backswing. The most common result is that the swing is late in relation to the cadence.

Hold your ball 2 feet lower than the usual extension setup position. This should place the ball at a level between your waist and knees. On count "one," let the ball swing freely, and continue your cadence. Compare this error with a swing from the correct height and see if you have a tendency to bend over and "help" the ball reach the top of the backswing.

b. *Feeling a clip.* A clip is the act of stopping the backswing short with the muscles of the shoulder and upper arm before it reaches the top of the backswing on its own. Common causes of the clip are a high or early pushaway, or limited flexibility of the shoulder. The most common result is that the swing is early in relation to the cadence.

Hold your ball 1 foot higher than the usual extension setup position, putting the ball at a level above the level of your shoulders. Remain erect. When you signal to begin the swing by saying "one," let the ball swing freely, and continue your cadence. Compare this error with a swing from the correct height and see if you have a tendency to stop the ball from freely going up to the top of the backswing.

**Success Goal =**

a. Compare 3 hoist swings with 3 free-pendulum swings ___

b. Compare 3 clip swings with 3 free-pendulum swings ___

**Success Check**

- Count cadence ___
- Adjust ball's height on "one" ___
- Hoist the ball by lifting it up behind you ___
- Clip the ball by stopping it short in your backswing ___

**To Increase Difficulty**

- Compare the interaction of high and low pushaway positions with muscling the ball (hoisting or clipping).

**To Decrease Difficulty**

- Use a lighter-weight ball.
- Ask a partner to hold your ball in an extended setup position to do this drill.

## 8. Swing Alignment Awareness

This drill introduces two errors in *swing plane* alignment (path of the ball in the swing), so that you can feel their effects on your body stabilization while you take no steps. Take a normal setup otherwise, returning to a two-handed setup after the backswing.

a. *Feeling a bumpout (convergent) swing.* The bumpout swing is usually caused by pushing the ball to a position directly in front of the body's centerline. The swing begins too far toward front and center, so the ball swings back to the outside (see Figure a).

From your setup position, push your ball 6 to 8 inches farther to the *inside* than in the extended pushaway position. Your ball will be almost directly in front of your body's centerline. Remain squared otherwise; do not turn your bowling shoulder inward.

When ready, start your cadence. On count "one," let the ball swing freely. Compare this error with properly directed swings to feel the difference.

b. *Feeling a wraparound (divergent) swing.* A wraparound swing is usually caused by pushing the ball too far to the outside. The ball swings back behind the center of the body (see Figure b).

From your setup position, push your ball 6 to 8 inches farther to the *outside* than in the extended pushaway position. This action should place the ball 6 to 8 inches to the outside of your ideal swing plane. Remain squared otherwise; do not turn your bowling shoulder outward.

When ready, start your cadence. On count "one," let the ball swing freely. Compare this error with properly directed swings to feel the difference.

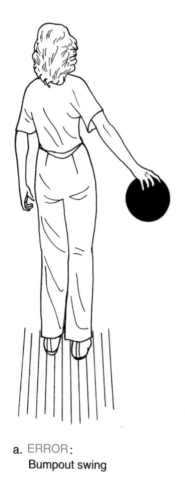

a. ERROR:
Bumpout swing

b. ERROR:
Wraparound swing

 **Success Goal** =

a. Compare 3 bumpout swings with 3 free-pendulum swings ___

b. Compare 3 wraparound swings with 3 free-pendulum swings ___

✔ **Success Check**

- Count cadence ___
- A bumpout swing pulls you off balance to the back and toward your swingside ___
- A wraparound swing pulls you off balance to the front and toward your balance side ___

**To Increase Difficulty**

- Try to feel any differences in your balance and posture when swinging the ball using a random order from the 3 different pushaway destinations: straight from shoulder, to inside, or to outside.

**To Decrease Difficulty**

- Use a lighter-weight ball.
- Ask a partner to hold your ball in an extended setup position to do this drill.

## 9. Takeaway Coordination

Another way to improve your balance during your swing is to extend your free arm, or balance arm. Start in a setup position. Push away to your extended arm position by count "one." As your ball begins to fall, execute the takeaway—remember to point your balance arm out, down, and back—as if to the wall (see Figure 2.4b). Your balance hand should be in its final position on your count of "two," and should remain outstretched in this position during counts of "three" (ball at top of backswing) and "four" (ball passing the swingside leg during the forward swing). Return to the normal setup position.

**Success Goal** = 10 consecutive coordinated swings and takeaways ___

✔ **Success Check**

- Start moving balance arm as ball falls into its swing ___
- Hold arm position during counts "two," "three," and "four" ___

**To Increase Difficulty**

- Close eyes to focus on exact timing.

**To Decrease Difficulty**

- Ask a partner to hold the ball in an extended setup position to start this drill.
- Ask partner to verbally count cadence.

## 10. High and Low Takeaway Awareness

This drill shows you how two improper takeaway positions feel, better preparing you for correcting such errors quickly. Set up as in the previous drill. Now, however, deliberately change your takeaway position to an incorrect one and ask yourself whether you feel more or less stable and whether your shoulders feel uneven. Each time, return to the normal setup position.

a. *Feeling a high takeaway.* When the ball begins to go into the downswing at the count of "one," move your balance hand to a position approximately 1 foot higher than the level of its shoulder (see Figure a). Concentrate on the effects of this error on the position of your swingside shoulder. Alternate with correct takeaways to sense the differences.

b. *Feeling a low takeaway.* When the ball begins to go into the downswing at the count of "one," move your balance hand directly to your balance side, with your hand almost touching the side of your upper leg (see Figure b). Concentrate on the effects of this error on the position of your swingside shoulder. Alternate with correct takeaways to sense the differences.

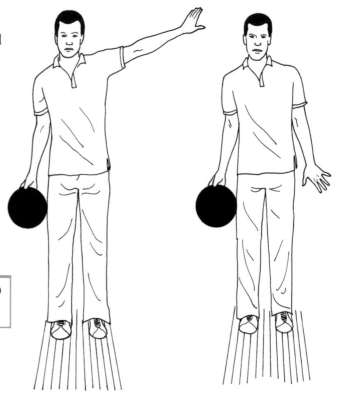

a. ERROR:
High takeaway

b. ERROR:
Low takeaway

### Success Goal =

a. Compare 5 high with 5 correct takeaways and swings __

b. Compare 5 low with 5 correct takeaways and swings __

### ✔ Success Check

• Shoulders square with correct takeaway __
• Shoulders level with correct takeaway __

### To Increase Difficulty

• Vary order of execution.

### To Decrease Difficulty

• Work with a partner from an extended setup position.

## 11. Front and Back Takeaway Awareness

As with the previous drill, the objective here is to deviate deliberately from the correct takeaway position so that you can study how the errors feel. Start with and return to the normal setup position.

a. *Feeling a front takeaway.* When the ball begins to go into the downswing at the count of "one," move your balance hand to a position in front of its shoulder, as if you were reaching for something (see Figure a). Concentrate on the effects of this error on the position of your swingside shoulder. Alernate with correct takeaways to sense the differences.

b. *Feeling a back takeaway.* When the ball begins to go into the backswing at the count of "one," move your balance hand to a position directly behind the hip of the sliding leg (see Figure b). Concentrate on the effects of this error on the position of your swingside shoulder during the swing. Alternate with correct takeaways to sense the differences.

a. ERROR:
Front takeaway

b. ERROR:
Back takeaway

### Success Goal =

a. Compare 5 front with 5 correct takeaways and swings ___

b. Compare 5 back with 5 correct takeaways and swings ___

### Success Check

• Start moving takeaway hand after count "one" ___

• Hold correctly placed takeaway position on counts "two," "three," and "four" ___

### To Increase Difficulty

• Close eyes to focus on shoulder position and balance effects.

### To Decrease Difficulty

• Work with a partner from an extended setup position.

## 12. Upper Body Coordination

Make sure that you can smoothly combine three movements in rhythm with your cadence: pushaway, pendulum swing, and takeaway (review Figure 2.4). Assume a normal setup position. Mentally count your swing cadence. Get ready to push on the "and." Push your ball into its extended arm position by count "one," let gravity start the downswing, and move your balance hand into its out, down, and back position. The ball should reach the bottom of your swing on count "two," the top of your backswing on count "three," and pass your swingside leg again on count "four." Begin to move your balance hand so that it will meet the ball returning to its extended position, then place your balance hand underneath the ball as you return to the normal setup position.

**Success Goal** = 5 consecutive coordinated upper body swings ___

### ✔ Success Check

- Feel elbows lock ___
- Feel ball fall into swing ___
- Move balance hand at same speed as the ball ___
- Hold balance arm outstretched ___

### To Increase Difficulty

- Ask a partner to count your cadence verbally, checking your consistency.

### To Decrease Difficulty

- Work with a partner from an extended arm position.

## SWING AND CADENCE SUCCESS SUMMARY

You have learned to contrast the feeling of a relaxed pendulum swing with various errors that can interfere with your future success. At the end of the pushaway, your swing arm must be sufficiently relaxed at the shoulder, your back and shoulders remaining stable; gravity can do the work of moving the ball through the swing. To make sure that you retain these desirable characteristics and correctly coordinate three movements (pushaway, free-pendulum swing, and takeaway), ask your teacher, coach, or a trained observer to qualitatively evaluate your technique according to the Keys to Success checklist items within Figure 2.5.

# STEP 3

# FOOTWORK: MATCHING YOUR CADENCE

During a bowling delivery there is no good reason to walk in any way other than taking a walk in the park or walking to the grocery store! Probably the best example of good footwork among professional bowlers is Mike Durbin. You probably have several bowlers at your local lanes who also look smooth on their approaches. Observe them closely, and you'll notice that these bowlers take heel-to-toe steps—identical to the way they normally walk. Heel-to-toe steps are preferred to shuffling steps because they allow a heel to touch down at the exact instant of a count, keeping the timing sharp and easier to troubleshoot.

One point should be emphasized with respect to timing: you must fit your footwork to your swing—not the other way around. The cadence you established with your pendulum swing gives you the pace for executing your footwork. However, you will first learn the footwork without swinging the ball.

## Why Is Footwork Important?

The pace of your footwork and the *mechanics of your gait*—the stepping pattern you use when you walk to the foul line—can help you establish the timing, balance, and strong finish that you'll need to stay coordinated during the delivery and effectively impart force to the ball at the finish (when practiced in Step 4).

### Timing

Heel-to-toe footwork synchronized with the swing cadence is more consistent and allows the force generated by the swing to peak on each step. When a bowler becomes tense (or *aroused*, an increase in *state anxiety)*, a common reaction is to increase the pace of the footwork, a condition called *fast feet*. Fast feet cause the ball to be late with respect to the footwork,

and the bowler falls victim to various problems caused by a late ball. Fast feet are difficult for bowlers to sense, because their attention is usually focused on a visual target (what the bowler looks at during the delivery).

### Balance

Heel-to-toe footwork allows better contact of your feet with a solid surface (the approach) and keeps your center of gravity over the center of a stable base of support. Any side-to-side stepping pattern deviation (see Figure 3.1, a-c) influences your ability to stay balanced; the more normal your stepping pattern, the better balanced you are (see Figure 3.1d).

### Finish

The way you walk to the foul line—the mechanics of your gait, has a great bearing upon your ability to put yourself in a high-leverage position (in which you can impart more rotation to the ball with your fingers). A relatively normal walking gait will prepare you for a superior finish position, which includes the slide, release, and follow-through. A superior finish position allows you to hit your target more often and to get more *pin action* (collisions of the pins) upon ball impact. Greater pin action results from *ball projection* (the ball goes further down the lane before it begins to roll and hook), which is maximized when the fingers lift the ball up and out and onto the lane surface while the hand is on the upswing. This movement is made easier from a bent-knee and an upright-back position.

## How to Execute Footwork

Take your position on the approach for a normal setup position. Do not insert your fingers into the

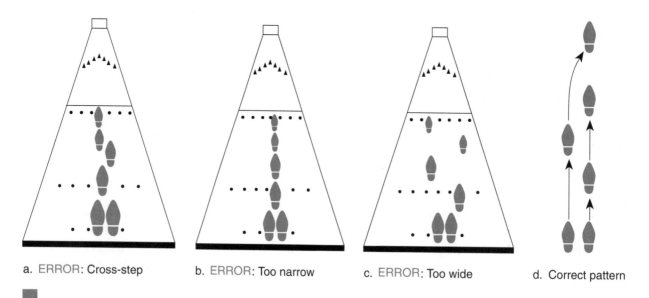

a. ERROR: Cross-step     b. ERROR: Too narrow     c. ERROR: Too wide     d. Correct pattern

**Figure 3.1** Three step pattern deviations: (a) cross-step, (b) too narrow, (c) too wide, and (d) the correct step pattern.

grip holes; rather, hold your ball with both hands at your midline, waist-level and touching your body; keep the ball against your body throughout the following foot movements. Next, start counting your cadence.

After establishing your rhythm, begin your first step forward on the "and" before "one," so that the heel of your swingside foot touches down on the count of "one" (see Figure 3.2a). Keep walking in a heel-to-toe fashion in rhythm with your cadence, holding your ball firmly at your midline. Touch down your sliding-foot heel on "two" (see Figure 3.2b).

On "three" touch down your swingside heel on the approach (see Figure 3.2c); it will be the anchor against which to push your balance-side *(sliding)* foot forward in the *slide* to the foul line. Immediately after count "three," begin deeply bending your swingside knee.

On "four" touch down your sliding foot sole and continue to push forward, using your swingside foot as the anchor. Keep your back upright and let your hips move down as your swingside foot remains anchored and your sliding foot moves forward, increasing the distance between your feet (see Figure 3.2d).

Your recovery position should be similar to that used by a skier landing after a distance jump or by a fencer during a lunge. This posture is termed *sitting tall.* It is described as (a) your back being upright, with no more than 20 degrees of forward lean; (b) your sliding leg being bent approximately 90 degrees, with its foot positioned under your body's center of gravity; (c) your swingside leg being extended back, almost straight, with the sole of this foot in the same place on the approach as when the slide began; and (d) your shoulders and hips being parallel with each other and perpendicular to the follow-through. Remember the meaning of the term *sitting tall.*

**FIGURE 3.2** **KEYS TO SUCCESS**

# FOOTWORK

a

b

c

## Count One

1. Midline ball setup ___
2. Count cadence ___
3. Swingside knee up on "and" ___
4. Back upright ___
5. Shoulders square ___
6. Swingside heel down on "one" ___

## Count Two

7. Sliding leg knee up ___
8. Sliding leg heel down on "two" ___

## Count Three

9. Swingside knee up ___
10. Anchor swingside heel on "three" ___

d

## Count Four

11. Sliding leg knee up ___
12. Sliding sole down on "four" ___
13. Push into slide ___
14. Sit tall ___
15. Anchor swingside foot ___

## FOOTWORK SUCCESS STOPPERS

You can eliminate most footwork errors if you learn how to recognize them before they become deeply ingrained. Some common errors and suggestions on how to correct them follow.

| Error | Correction |
| --- | --- |
| 1. You take steps too fast. | 1. Count through your cadence before you initiate movement. Fit your steps to the cadence. |
| 2. You take the first step on your toe or with a shuffle. | 2. Step out by lifting your foot off the approach just as you would if you were taking a walk. Think to yourself, "knee up." |
| 3. Your entire approach is made up of shuffling steps. | 3. Keep your legs straighter; do not bend your knees before beginning the fourth step and slide. Think "walk tall, heel-to-toe." |
| 4. Your heels touch down too abruptly, with the sole of each shoe slapping. | 4. Do not lock your knees; walk in your normal fashion to the line. |
| 5. You walk too wide a track, too narrow a track, or in a cross-stepping pattern. | 5. Allow your feet to trace a path slightly inside each hip and parallel with your swing. Also, check to see that your pushaway is directed in line with your shoulder and the target. |
| 6. You are off balance at the foul line. | 6. Keep your back straight, with your swingside knee bending deeply as you push your slide toward the foul line. Think, "sit tall." |

# DRILLS

These drills begin from the midline ball setup position. After taking your position on the approach for a normal setup, remember not to put your fingers in the holes or align the ball with your swing plane. Just hold your ball in both hands at your midline, waist-level and touching your body.

*Courtesy Tip*: You are slowly and systematically performing these drills and may be quite visible to others bowling nearby. Always check for clearance on either side of you, just as you would when bowling a normal game.

## 1. Footwork and Cadence

Take the midline ball setup at your normal setup location at the back of the approach. Begin counting your cadence.

On the "and" count, step out with your swingside foot. On "one" touch the swingside heel down on the approach. Take normal heel-to-toe walking steps and concentrate on the feeling of your weight being transferred from the heel, through the arch, and to the toe as you walk forward. Make your motions flow smoothly.

On the count of "two," touch your sliding foot heel down on the approach.

On "three" make sure to keep your knees straight and anchor your swingside heel on the approach in preparation for a push into the finish position. Notice the feeling of walking tall.

On "four" push your sliding foot forward, using your swingside foot as the anchor on the approach. Bend your swingside knee deeply as you slide.

*Mental Picture*: At the finish, you are on a tightrope; your swingside foot is pushing your sliding foot along. Your back is upright, both knees are bent, your eyes are looking down the rope, and your chest and shoulders are perpendicular to the rope.

**Success Goal** = To match your footwork to your swing's cadence (without doing a pendulum swing) ___

✔ **Success Check**
• Begin step on "and" ___
• Heel touches on first three cadence counts ___
• Bend swingside knee deeply after "three" ___
• Push sliding foot forward ___
• Anchor with sole of swingside foot ___
• Hold sitting tall position ___

**To Increase Difficulty**
• Compare the effects of walking faster and slower on your balance. Deliberately count a faster, then a slower, cadence before you start walking. Learn just how fast or slow your limits of good balance are.

**To Decrease Difficulty**
• Do only the push off your swingside foot a few times to get the feel of the power needed to slide forward into the finish position. Use the cues "and," "three," "and," "push" (for "four").
• Slowly take your steps one at a time, gradually increasing tempo to match your cadence speed.

## 2. Starting Position Check

After achieving some footwork consistency in the previous drill, you are now ready to make a precise determination of how far from the foul line you should start your approach. The conventional method is to pace off four normal walking steps and add a half step for the slide, but this method is undesirable because it does not allow enough room for a sufficiently long push and slide.

Perform the previous footwork drill again, noting how far your sliding toe stops from the foul line each time. Mark this location off to one side with a ruler, piece of paper, or other small object. (Be careful not to step on it and slip.)

After several repetitions, checking the quality of your footwork and push, and repositioning the marker each time, measure the distance of the marker from the foul line. Walk back to your original starting position and establish your new starting position this distance closer to the foul line.

From this new position, make five more footwork trials ending with the push; see how close your sliding toe is to the foul line. If necessary, adjust your starting position to allow your sliding toe to stop 2 to 4 inches from the line. Remember this new position well; write it down if necessary. This will be your new starting position.

Take 10 well-executed footwork patterns, giving yourself one point for each time your sliding foot stops within 4 inches from the foul line.

**Success Goal** = To identify your personal starting position ___

**Success Check**
- Repeat footwork with your cadence ___
- Measure distance from sliding toe to foul line ___
- Sliding toe 2 to 4 inches from foul line ___
- Check quality of footwork ___
- Establish new starting position ___

**To Increase Difficulty**
- Use a variety of starting positions, and notice how these positions affect your normal walking pattern to avoid touching the foul line at the end of your approach. Usually a position too far from the foul line will result in the heels touching down too abruptly; a position too close will result in the inability to stretch out (assume a low position) sufficiently during the slide.

**To Decrease Difficulty**
- Have a practice partner assist you with measurements.

## FOOTWORK SUCCESS SUMMARY

Before you attempt to add any upper-body movements to the footwork, you must be sure that you are (1) taking heel-to-toe steps, (2) matching your steps with your cadence, and (3) pushing to a strong, well-balanced finish position without crossing the foul line. To help you sharpen these skills, ask your teacher, coach, or a practice partner to evaluate your technique according to the checklist items within Figure 3.2.

# STEP 4

# FOUR-STEP DELIVERY: BOWLING THE BALL

Y ou're liable to see all different "styles" of bowling form, from three to eight steps, a crouching posture, duck-walking footwork, little or no backswing, or a very high backswing. You can use any form to knock down the pins, sometimes scoring quite high! In short, any style will work—for a price! The price is a lack of consistency and greater wear and tear on the body. The complicated form takes much practice and causes imbalance of muscles from side to side. A more reliable, four-step delivery is described as the natural delivery (even though there is really no *natural* way to deliver a bowling ball). In addition, the four-step delivery is the core of the five-step delivery (not covered in this book). Once you know how to do the four-step delivery, you're ready to bowl and score your own games.

## Why Is the Four-Step Delivery Important?

A four-step delivery is important because it contains the least number of steps you can take to allow an unhurried pushaway and a free pendulum swing within a normal walking pace. A consistent, well-coordinated delivery represents your best technique, the most efficient thing you do in bowling. It contains no wasted movements, tires you less, and allows for fewer opportunities to commit errors throughout the delivery. A four-step delivery helps you coordinate your footwork (lower-body movements) with your swing timing (upper-body movements).

Unfortunately, many bowlers spend a lifetime of bowling trying to fit their footwork patterns to swings that are neither consistent nor free. Remember, a short arm has a short-timed pendulum swing. The ball will take less time to move through the arc of the short swing than through the arc of a person with a longer arm. Hence, the footwork may be taken more quickly. A longer arm, and the resulting longer-timed swing, requires slower footwork.

## How to Make a Four-Step Delivery

A four-step delivery consists of

- a pushaway coordinated with the first step,
- a free-pendulum swing,
- a takeaway coordinated with the pendulum swing,
- heel-to-toe steps timed to fit the pendulum swing, and
- a high leverage "power push" finish.

These five elements are combined into a coordinated, smoothly flowing motion of delivering the ball—the *four-step delivery*.

Assume a normal setup at the appropriate location at the back of the approach. Use a heel-to-toe walking pattern; remember not to place one foot in front of the other as in walking a straight line, not to step side to side, and not to cross one foot in front of the other (see Figure 3.1, p. 40). Concentrate on the feel of your weight being transferred from the heel, through the arch, and to the toe as you walk forward. Make all of your movements flow together into one graceful sequence.

Begin counting your cadence: "AND one AND two AND three AND four AND one" (and so on).

*On the "and" after "four"*: Begin pushing your ball straight forward (never down) with both hands and in line with your bowling shoulder and your target. Keep your bowling arm 90 degrees (perpendicular) to your shoulders.

*On "one"*: Step forward with your swingside foot so that your elbows lock (extend into the pushaway position) as your swingside heel makes contact simultaneously on the count of "one" (see Figure 4.1a).

Proper timing of the pushaway with the swingside foot in the first step is necessary to create a free-pendulum swing and to establish proper timing for the entire delivery. *This is the most important and difficult coordinated movement you will make in bowling. You must do it correctly every time; you will always have to think about what you are doing during the first step and pushaway—whether in practice or competition.* The benefits of doing so will be great, because the rest of your delivery will be less troublesome.

*On the "and" after "one"*: Let your ball fall into the downswing from the extended arm position (the pushaway) and let your balance arm move to an out, down, and back position (the takeaway) at the same speed as the ball falling into the downswing. Lift your sliding foot; keep walking—do not hesitate.

*On "two:"* Your sliding foot heel makes contact on "two." Keep walking; do not bend your knees. Your ball should be at its lowest point in the downswing (see Figure 4.1b), and the takeaway is in position.

*On the "and" after "two"*: Begin your third heel-to-toe step with your swingside foot.

*On "three"*: Let your swingside foot heel make contact, preparing this foot for pushing the sliding foot. This is the longest step; do not bend your knees yet. Your ball should be at the top of the backswing, neither moving up nor coming down. Keep your upper body upright (keep your head back) and do not bend over at the waist (see Figure 4.1c).

*On the "and" after "three"*: Begin to lift your sliding foot off the approach.

*On "four"*: Your ball should be at its lowest point in the forward swing. Deeply bend your swingside

knee as you touch down the toe of your sliding foot on the approach. Push your sliding foot forward, using your swingside foot as an anchor (see Figure 4.1d). Lower your hips; keep your back upright and your shoulders stable as your ball moves in the forward swing, from the top of the backswing to the release point.

The finish is the coordinated movement of your upper and lower body that begins with your swingside heel touching down (in preparation for the slide) and ends with the completed follow-through. The objective is to get the ball and the sliding foot moving together unhurried toward the foul line. A high-quality finish allows consistently accurate projection of your ball onto the lane with more power because you use the larger and stronger muscles of your back and legs to do the job while you hold your shoulders perpendicular to your swing plane. Look for the feeling of being in time and well balanced during the delivery, and of good leverage during your release.

During your release, keep your wrist firm. Your thumb should exit the ball just before the ball passes your center of gravity (at the bottom of the forward swing), and your fingers should continue to lift the ball onto the lane surface (to project it) and exit after the ball passes your center of gravity. Keep your swingside sole anchored firmly where it was when you began your slide, keep your hips and shoulders perpendicular to your swing, and keep your back straight, almost perpendicular to the approach. Maintain this pose at the foul line until the ball is at least halfway down the lane; maintain the balance of the sitting tall position (see Figure 4.1e).

FIGURE
4.1  **KEYS TO SUCCESS**

# FOUR-STEP DELIVERY
### Count "and" after "four"

1. Push ball out from shoulder to target ____
2. Step forward with swingside foot ____
3. Keep shoulders square ____
4. Keep head and shoulders back ____

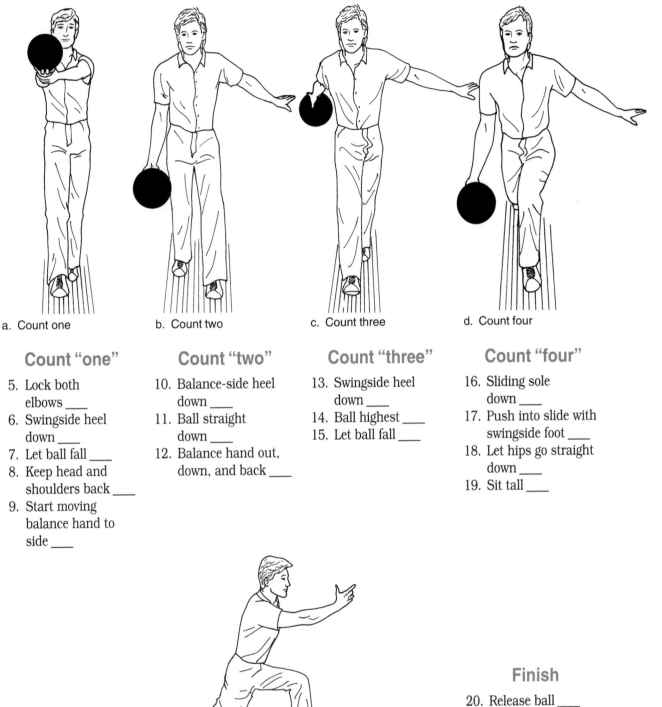

a. Count one

b. Count two

c. Count three

d. Count four

### Count "one"

5. Lock both elbows ___
6. Swingside heel down ___
7. Let ball fall ___
8. Keep head and shoulders back ___
9. Start moving balance hand to side ___

### Count "two"

10. Balance-side heel down ___
11. Ball straight down ___
12. Balance hand out, down, and back ___

### Count "three"

13. Swingside heel down ___
14. Ball highest ___
15. Let ball fall ___

### Count "four"

16. Sliding sole down ___
17. Push into slide with swingside foot ___
18. Let hips go straight down ___
19. Sit tall ___

e. Finish

### Finish

20. Release ball ___
21. Follow through high ___
22. Hold final position ___

## FOUR-STEP DELIVERY SUCCESS STOPPERS

Good bowling is nothing more than making the best shot (delivery) that you can and immediately correcting any errors on your very next shot—"keeping your head in the game!" You can make consistently better shots if you learn how to recognize and correct the following errors in your four-step delivery.

| Error | Correction |
|---|---|
| 1. You take your first step on the toe or with a shuffle. | 1. Step out by lifting the foot off the approach just as you would if you were taking a walk. Think to yourself, "heel-to-toe." |
| 2. Your ball arrives later than your sliding foot at the foul line or your ball drops before the desired release point, or you feel yourself imparting excessive lift with your fingers at the release. | 2. To correct for a late pushaway, push the ball faster, not sooner than your first step. Be sure to start moving the ball and your foot at the same instant, but not at the same speed. |
| 3. Your ball arrives at the foul line before your sliding foot, or you hop (take a quick step) between the second and third steps, or you feel as if there is no lift with your fingers at the release. | 3. To correct for an early pushaway, begin pushing the ball as you begin to move your foot. Regulate the speed of the pushaway so that the ball reaches the locked-elbows position as the heel touches down on the count of "one." |
| 4. Your upper body follows the ball forward in the pushaway. | 4. Keep the muscles of your spine rigid to counteract the weight of the ball moving forward. Think to yourself, "walk tall and be snooty." |
| 5. You step on your heel, not slide, forward to the foul line. | 5. When your ball reaches the top of the backswing, step forward on your toe, slide forward; do not lift your sliding foot off the approach. |
| 6. You drop your bowling shoulder. | 6. Keep your shoulders level; stretch your balance arm out, down, and back. |
| 7. You "double bounce" the ball (hit the approach with the ball before you have released it). | 7. Do not lean over; keep your shoulders straight and take it easy. Lower your hips gently; do not lunge. |
| 8. You loft the ball (hold on too long and toss it too far out into the lane). | 8. Simply let your ball swing down on its own. Keep your wrist firm; do not squeeze the grip. |
| 9. You lose balance and step over to your swingside after the release. | 9. Bend your swingside leg more deeply as you slide forward. |

**FOUR-STEP DELIVERY**

# DRILLS
### 1. Trial Delivery

In this drill, you'll merge your footwork with your swing, particularly focusing on the timing of your first step.

Assume a normal setup position on the approach. Begin by counting your cadence. On the "and" after "four," begin your push and your step; push your bowling arm out crisply with your balance hand. On "one," let your swingside foot's heel contact the approach, and lock both elbows at the extended position (the pushaway). Concentrate on the imaginary click of your elbows, the real tap of your swingside heel, and the arrival of your ball in the pushaway occurring at the same instant (perfect timing; see Figure a).

Then, let your ball fall into its pendulum swing as you continue your footwork to complete a trial delivery. At this point, do not be concerned with the number of actual pins knocked down.

**Success Goal** = To feel the correct timing between your pushaway and first step during a trial delivery ___

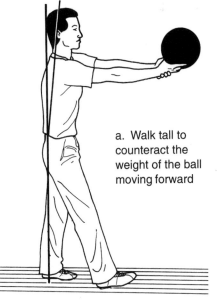

a. Walk tall to counteract the weight of the ball moving forward

✔ **Success Check**

| Step | Ball position | Foot in front |
|------|---------------|---------------|
| • 1 | Straight out in front ___ | Swingside (heel down) ___ |
| • 2 | Straight down ___ | Balance side (heel down) ___ |
| • 3 | Straight out in back ___ | Swingside (heel down) ___ |
| • 4 (slide) | Straight down ___ | Balance side (toe down) ___ |

**To Increase Difficulty**

- Deliberately delay your pushaway so you can study the feel by waiting until the count of "one" to begin your pushaway.
- Deliberately force a premature pushaway (before you start your first step) so you can study the feel by waiting until the count of "one" to step out with your swingside foot.

**To Decrease Difficulty**

- Without a ball, work with a partner face to face. Stand as if you were holding a ball, approximately 2 to 3 feet away from your partner. Your partner should hold one palm up, like a traffic officer signaling a stop, 2 to 3 inches higher than your hands in your setup position. Your partner's open palm represents your pushaway destination (see Figure b).
- With a ball, work with a partner face to face. Make sure that your partner is ready to accept your ball prior to starting your cadence. Coincide the ball's arrival in your partner's hands with your swingside heel's contact on the approach.

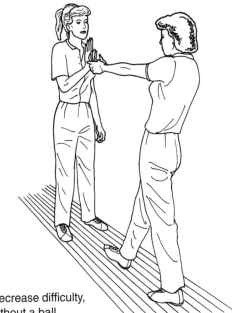

b. To decrease difficulty, work without a ball

## 2. One-Step Delivery

This drill may also be called a "finish" or a "power push" delivery. You should practice your finish often for two main reasons. First, you can use it to help you analyze, troubleshoot, and ingrain movements. Second, you can use it to strengthen and maintain the back, leg, and hand muscles involved in giving your delivery more power.

Assume your normal setup position, but stand approximately 4 feet from the foul line, facing the second arrow. Begin your cadence and focus on your visual target.

Execute every movement above the waist as in a normal delivery; however, take no steps. Push the ball and let it fall into its free-pendulum swing (see Figure a). On the "and" after "three," when your ball is starting its forward swing, begin lifting your sliding foot off the approach.

*Note*: What happens during an actual delivery when you bend your knees before the count of "three"? This is known as *premature bend*, and it shortens your third step. The swingside sole would be the only part of the foot in contact with the approach prior to your push. Thus, your foot would slip, coming off the approach and into the air. Your hips (and shoulders) would turn away from the swing, depriving you of valuable leverage.

When your ball is at its lowest point in the forward swing, on the count of "four," say "push" to yourself and make your sliding sole contact the approach in its step forward; your swingside knee should still be bending. Using your swingside sole as an anchor, push your sliding foot forward toward the foul line (see Figure b). Keep your upper body almost perpendicular to the approach (not bent over more than 20 degrees), and allow your center of gravity (roughly your hips) to move down toward the approach. Release your ball on the upswing, keeping the same speed (see Figure c).

*Note*: You may have difficulty maintaining traction with your swingside foot if the sole is not made of rubber or if it has a leather tip. If this is the case, have a professional shoe repairer cover the entire sole with nonmarring rubber. Do not use plastic, neoprene, or sponge crepe; gummy rubber like "Louisana crepe" is acceptable.

In your final resting, or recovery, position, hold the sitting tall position, with the entire sole and heel of your sliding shoe and the front half of the sole of your swingside shoe still in contact with the approach. Hold your back upright, as it was in your initial setup position.

a

b

c

**Success Goal** = 2 out of 3 consecutive one-step deliveries with control and correct timing ___

**Success Check**
- Back upright ___
- Pushaway straight out ___
- Takeaway and downswing in time ___
- Begin push against back foot on "and" after "three" ___
- Begin slide on "four" ___
- Ball and slide in time ___
- Project ball onto lane ___
- Sit tall ___
- High follow-through ___

**To Increase Difficulty**
- Try to "line up" and hit a target. First, put your shoulder over the 10th board (second arrow board), look at the second arrow, and take the one-step delivery trying to roll your ball over the second arrow. When your ball hits the second arrow, notice where it contacts the pins and move your feet, 2 boards at a time, in the same direction of where the ball missed the pocket. Repeat until your ball is hitting the pocket. Try to hit the pocket as many times in a row as you can. Do not attempt your spares; sweep remaining pins off of the pin deck.

**To Decrease Difficulty**
- Ask your partner to watch you. Compare your recall of your execution and timing with your partner's assessment.

## 3. Four-Step Delivery

Assume a normal setup and mentally count your cadence. Review the Keys to Success checklist items within Figure 4.1, then try them. Take all steps at the same pace, not hesitating between steps. Use a heel-to-toe walking pattern. Make all of your movements flow together into one graceful sequence. Concentrate on the feeling of being in time during the delivery and on the feeling of good leverage during your push toward the foul line. Do not worry if you feel awkward; keep trying, and your movements will become more comfortable.

**Success Goal** = To correctly time your four-count delivery with your cadence ___

**Success Check**
- Use heel-to-toe walking steps ___
- Make steps fluid ___
- Adjust footwork to match your cadence ___
- Hold final follow-through pose ___

**To Increase Difficulty**
- Increase the number of deliveries; stop when tired or when you begin to experience a loss of coordination.
- Try to hit the pocket as many times in a row as you can (review the directions on how to "line up" from the previous drill's "To Increase Difficulty" section).

**To Decrease Difficulty**
- Use no ball and walk more slowly.
- Use a lighter-weight ball.

## 4. Incorrect Pushaway Destination

Learn the effects of four common pushaway destination errors on your delivery. Refer to Step 2, Drills 1-3, 7, and 8 for techniques without footwork. In this drill, you will set up for a normal delivery and deliberately use incorrect pushaway destinations to study how you feel during the delivery.

*Vertical errors.* Errors in the vertical level (height) of the pushaway change the timing relationship of your swing to your footwork. If your pushaway is too high, the ball is placed into the swing plane later than the footwork (behind the feet); if your pushaway is too low, the ball is placed into the swing earlier than the footwork (ahead of the feet).

*Lateral errors.* A misaligned pushaway causes a misaligned swing, pulling you off balance and making it difficult to control your center of gravity. Errors in the lateral direction of the pushaway are unnoticed and persistent, and they can cause your ball to miss the target and the point of pin impact. If not corrected, they can lessen the ability of your ball to strike on apparently good hits.

For each of the following deviations, begin counting in your setup. On the "and" after "four," step out with your swingside foot and begin to push the ball to the indicated pushaway destination. On "one," lock your elbows at the extended position and continue your delivery.

a. *Excessively high pushaway.* Destination: 1 to 2 feet higher than the correct level. Repeat this type of pushaway 5 times, alternating with 5 correct pushaways, noting the comparative effects of this error. With the high pushaway, you may *clip* your backswing, stopping it short before the ball reaches the top of the backswing on its own.

b. *Excessively low pushaway.* Destination: 1 to 2 feet lower than the correct level. Repeat this type of pushaway 5 times, alternating with 5 correct pushaways, noting the comparative effects of this error. Because the ball does not have enough momentum of its own, you may *hoist* your backswing, raising the ball to a level higher than the pushaway destination. In this case, your ball is ahead of your footwork, and you hoist your backswing in an attempt to allow your feet time to get ahead of the ball before the last step, slide, and release.

c. *Inside (convergent) pushaway.* Destination: 6 to 8 inches farther to the inside than the correct location (see Figure a). Repeat this type of pushaway 5 times, alternating with 5 correct pushaways, noting the comparative effects of this error. Note the following: teetering of the upper body from side-to-side (being out of balance); a *bumpout* backswing, in which the ball moves away from your centerline in the back; and being somewhat cramped at the release, with the ball moving back toward your centerline.

d. *Outside (divergent) pushaway.* Destination: 6 to 8 inches farther to the outside than the correct location (see Figure b). Repeat this type of pushaway 5 times, alternating with 5 correct pushaways, noting the comparative effects of this error. Note the following: being off balance to the outside; a *wraparound* backswing, in which the ball moves toward your centerline in the back; and the need to reach to the outside during the forward swing and follow-through.

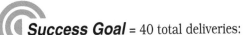

## Success Goal = 40 total deliveries:

a. Alternate 5 high with 5 correct pushaways ___

b. Alternate 5 low with 5 correct pushaways ___

c. Alternate 5 inside with 5 correct pushaways ___

d. Alternate 5 outside with 5 correct pushaways ___

## To Increase Difficulty

- Line up for a strike with your normal delivery. Then attempt to strike using each of the deviations.

## To Decrease Difficulty

- Begin by using no ball or a lighter ball.

## Success Check

- Count cadence ___
- Push ball on "and" after four ___
- Focus on correct pushaway execution ___

a. ERROR: Inside pushaway     b. ERROR: Outside pushaway

## 5. Late and Early Pushaway

Learn about two troublesome errors in pushaway timing. Late pushaway, or late ball timing, means that you push your ball out after your first step begins. Early pushaway, or early ball timing, means that you push your ball out before your first step begins. Refer to Step 2, Drill 1 for correct technique without footwork. In this drill, you will deliberately force pushaway timing errors so you can feel their effects on your normal delivery.

a. *Late Pushaway Awareness.* Begin counting in your setup. On the "and" after "four," step out with your swingside foot, but wait until the count of "one" to begin your pushaway. On "one," lock your elbows at the extended position and continue your delivery. Note any feeling of awkwardness. You may feel yourself accelerating the ball during the swing to catch up with your steps.

b. *Early Pushaway Awareness.* Begin counting in your setup. On the "and" after "four," begin your pushaway, but wait until the count of "one" to step out with your swingside foot. On "one," lock your elbows at the extended position and continue your delivery. Note any feeling of awkwardness. You may feel yourself being pulled forward by the ball because your center of gravity has moved to a point in front of your body. You may try to hoist your ball into the backswing and speed up your footwork to allow your feet to get ahead of your ball.

**Success Goal** = 20 total deliveries:

a. Alternate 5 late pushaways with 5 correctly timed pushaways ___

b. Alternate 5 early pushaways with 5 correctly timed pushaways ___

✔ **Success Check**

• Count cadence ___
• Push ball on "and" after four ___
• Concentrate on difference between error and correctness ___
• Complete delivery ___

**To Increase Difficulty**

• Line up for a strike with your normal delivery. Then attempt to strike using each of the incorrect timings.

**To Decrease Difficulty**

• Begin by using no ball or a lighter-weight ball.

## 6. Incorrect Takeaways

Learn how an incorrect takeaway affects your delivery. Refer to Step 2, Drills 9-11 for techniques without footwork. During a delivery, a correct takeaway keeps your shoulders perpendicular to your swing and level with the floor. To feel the effects, deliberately incorporate the following four errors into three or more successive deliveries: high, low, front, and back. Alternate these errors with correct takeaways to see what effects they have on body stability and the ball path.

**Success Goal** = 24 total deliveries:

a. Alternate 3 high takeaways with 3 correct takeaways ___

b. Alternate 3 low takeaways with 3 correct takeaways ___

c. Alternate 3 front takeaways with 3 correct takeaways ___

d. Alternate 3 back takeaways with 3 correct takeaways ___

**Success Check**

- Count cadence ___
- Begin takeaway after "one" ___
- Concentrate on difference between error and correctness ___
- Complete delivery ___

**To Increase Difficulty**

- Line up for a strike with your normal delivery, then attempt to strike using each of the incorrect takeaways.

**To Decrease Difficulty**

- Begin by using no ball or a lighter-weight ball.

## 7. Scoring a Game

Do you know how to keep score by hand? Today, so many establishments have automatic scoring devices that many bowlers never learn how to keep score. Review the text explanations on how to keep score.

A *mark* refers to a strike (notated by an X) or a spare (a slash, or diagonal line). A *miss*, or an *error* (a horizontal bar), means that pins were left standing after two attempts in the frame. The small boxes in the upper right corner of each game frame are reserved for recording the results of the deliveries in each single frame, such as first- and second-ball pin counts, marks, misses, *splits* (pins other than the headpin left standing with pins missing in between—designated by an open circle) and split *conversions* (spared split—designated by an open circle with a slash through it); the large area is reserved for entering the cumulative score.

A *strike* earns 10 pins for the frame in which it was bowled *plus* the pinfall from **the next two deliveries**. A *spare* earns 10 pins for the frame in which it was bowled *plus* the pinfall from the **next single delivery**. To score a strike or spare, place the appropriate symbol in the small box for the frame. Then you must wait until the next frame to add the cumulative score. Any frame without a strike or spare earns only the actual pinfall for the frame, and all score entries are made current through that frame.

To help you understand how to keep score, fill in the blank gameline frames according to the directions, after you read about each frame's action.

## Scorekeeping Exercise

**Frames 1, 2, and 3:** You strike in your 1st, 2nd, and 3rd frames.

**Score:** Mark the symbol for a strike in each of the first three frames. Write your score in the first frame; do not enter a score in the second frame or third frame yet.

**Frame 4:** Next you knock down five pins on your first ball (delivery) of the fourth frame and only three pins with your second ball.

**Score:** Write your score in all appropriate frames. (Hint: There should be numbers in the first four frames.)

**Frame 5:** You knock down seven pins with your first ball, leaving a split (i.e., two pins on one side of the lane and one pin on the other). You then knock down all the pins of the split, making your attempt a spare.

**Score:** Make all appropriate entries in the fifth frame. Do not forget to put the symbol for a spared split in the appropriate box. Wait until the first ball of the next frame to enter a numerical score.

**Frame 6:** You strike.

**Score:** Write your score in the fifth frame. Mark the symbol for a strike in the sixth frame, but do not insert a numerical score yet. (The term for this designation is a "strike up.")

**Frame 7, first ball:** You foul, getting zero for the ball, as if you had rolled it into the channel.

**Score:** Wait until your spare attempt before recording any score in the sixth frame, because your strike in the sixth frame allows you to count the next **two** deliveries toward the score in the sixth frame.

**Frame 7, second ball:** You knock down only nine pins on your spare attempt, which was shot at a full rack of pins.

**Score:** Write your cumulative scores in the sixth and seventh frames.

**Frame 8:** You knock down eight pins on the first ball of the eighth frame, then convert the spare.

**Score:** Make the appropriate entry in the eighth frame. (Hint: Because it contains a mark, there should be no numerical score in the eighth frame.)

**Frame 9:** You then leave two pins standing on your first ball of the ninth frame, adding eight pins to the spare in the eighth frame. However, you miss both pins on your spare attempt.

**Score:** Write in your scores in the eighth and the ninth frames.

**Frame 10:** You now strike on your first ball, allowing you to count the pinfall on it and the next two attempts. You strike again in the "eleventh," then get seven pins on your twelfth attempt.

**Score:** Make all appropriate entries through the tenth frame.

| NAME | HDCP | 1 | 2 | 3 | 4 | 5 | 6 | 7 | 8 | 9 | 10 |
|---|---|---|---|---|---|---|---|---|---|---|---|
| | | | | | | | | | | | |
| | | | | | | | | | | | |

**Success Goal** = Correctly score a game ___

✔ **Success Check**
- Complete score according to directions ___
- Check your score for accuracy ___

### To Increase Difficulty
- Pair up with a partner and separately score each other's game. Check your score either against your partner's score, or against the score kept by an automatic scoring device.
- Repeat this drill until you feel comfortable both with your four-step delivery and scoring a game.

### To Decrease Difficulty
- After each frame, compare your score either with your partner's score, or with an automatic scoring device.
- Work with a partner, helping each other to analyze and correct any differences in calculating scores.
- Limit a game to five frames and record your score.

**Answer Key to Scorekeeping Exercise**

| NAME | HDCP | 1 | 2 | 3 | 4 | 5 | 6 | 7 | 8 | 9 | 10 |
|------|------|---|---|---|---|---|---|---|---|---|----|
| Sue | | ⊠ | ⊠ | ⊠ 5 3 | 7 Ø | ⊠ | F 9 | 8 / | 8 – | ⊠ ⊠ 7 | |
| | | 30 | 55 | 73 | 81 | 101 | 120 | 129 | 147 | 155 | 182 |

## 8. 300 Drill

This drill involves scoring a game without actually counting the pins knocked down. Ask a partner to evaluate your ability to coordinate your upper-body movements (pushaway, pendulum swing, and takeaway) with your lower-body movements (footwork matching your swing cadence).

If you execute with correct timing on your first ball, mark a strike on your scoresheet. If you do not execute correct timing on your first ball, mark 5 points. If you execute with correct timing on your second ball, mark a spare. If you do not execute correct timing on your second ball, mark a miss. Tally your points to get as close as possible to a perfect "300" game.

**Success Goal** = 225 out of 300 possible points ___

✔ **Success Check**
- Follow Keys to Success Items in Figure 4.1 ___

### To Increase Difficulty
- Use two different game lines, one to record actual pins knocked down and a second one to tally your score according to execution points. Then, compare differences.

### To Decrease Difficulty
- Use a rating scale from 5 to 10 points to assign execution points for each delivery.

### 9. Scoring Multiple Games

To ingrain your four-step delivery technique, bowl and record your scores for at least 10 games. Total your 10 scores, then divide by 10 to get an average game score.

**Success Goal** = To chart your game scores over an extended time period ___

**Success Check**
• Follow the scoring rules ___
• Follow the Keys to Success in Figure 4.1 ___

**To Increase Difficulty**
• Troubleshoot to identify and correct any errors noticed.

**To Decrease Difficulty**
• Work with a partner to record scores and give each other feedback on technique.
• Assume each ball is a strike situation.

## FOUR-STEP DELIVERY SUCCESS SUMMARY

*Do not expect perfection, but always try for perfection!* Do not think that you have failed because you do not execute perfectly every time. The objective is to be as near perfect as possible, realizing that you will not be perfect; this is "staying sharp." In simply trying for perfection, you will keep your movements as close as possible to your internal standards of what the movements should feel like, allowing you performance well within the limits of usefulness. Thus, you can keep yourself under control, and bowl more consistently over a longer period of time.

To keep your delivery sharp and timed with your cadence, ask your teacher, coach, or a practice partner to evaluate your technique as often as necessary, according to the Keys to Success checklist items within Figure 4.1. Also, make sure that you know how to keep score.

# STEP 5

# BALL DYNAMICS: ROLLING STRAIGHT AND HOOK BALLS

To the novice bowler, one of the great mysteries is how the bowling ball knocks down all of the pins. The "heavy" roll of a ball delivered by Walter Ray Williams, Jr. and the often startling hook ball delivered by Pete Weber have kept avid spectators spellbound in recent years. The way their balls knock down the pins is quite spectacular. They are very skilled, however, in applying consistent dynamics to their balls; you can develop this kind of skill through knowledge, a lot of practice, and competition.

*Ball dynamics* are the collective skidding and rolling motions of a bowling ball as it proceeds down the lane toward the pins. The way a ball visibly acts on the lane is popularly called a *ball reaction.* Two reaction types are the *straight ball* and the *hook ball.*

The straight ball travels a straight path from your hand to the desired, or *object*, pin or to a point of impact with the pins. The straight ball will be introduced first because it is the best model for learning the high-leverage release, without the hand and arm positioning problems commonly encountered by inexperienced bowlers attempting to roll the hook.

The hook ball travels a bent, outside-to-inside path from your hand to the object pin. You should learn the hook ball after the straight ball so that you can systematically build your hook ball skills on those developed with the straight ball (see Figure 5.1a,b).

Two poor alternatives to the hook ball are often described in bowling texts; they are mentioned so that you can identify them. One is *the backup ball,* or *reverse hook,* and the other is the *curve ball* (see Figure 5.1c,d).

The backup ball veers from the bowler's inside to his or her outside. It is rolled with the fingers held pointed at approximately the 3 o'clock (9 o'clock for a left-handed bowler) position at the release (see Figure 5.2).

*Note*: The clock face terminology used in describing hand positions always refers to the direction in which the tips of the bowling fingers are pointing, not the thumb. To get the proper perspective, point

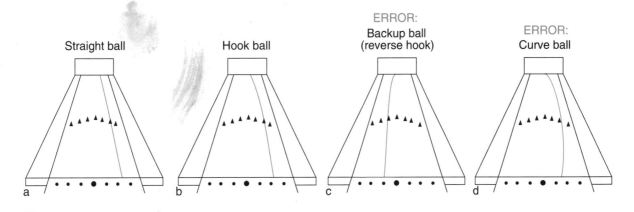

Straight ball     Hook ball     ERROR: Backup ball (reverse hook)     ERROR: Curve ball

a     b     c     d

**Figure 5.1** Four types of ball reaction (dynamics) for right-handed bowlers. Note: the backup and curve balls are incorrect.

59

ERROR: Backup ball

**Figure 5.2** Clock face diagram of hand position used to deliver a backup ball.

your bowling arm straight out from your shoulder and look down to your fingers as if you were taking aim with a rifle.

The curve ball no longer exists. It was rolled by turning the wrist from the outside to the inside at the instant of release (see Figure 5.3a,b). Although possible on oiled shellac- or lacquer-coated lane surfaces, its dynamics are not possible on present-day, oiled urethane lane surfaces.

Regardless of how the lane surface is coated, a ball used by the same bowler will develop a ball track. A *ball track* is a ring of nicks and scratches that de-

ERROR: Curve ball

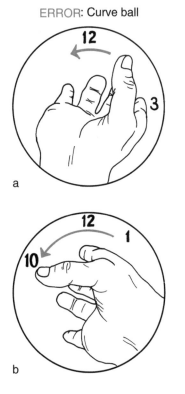

a

b

**Figure 5.3** Clock face diagrams of hand positions used to deliver a curve ball.

velop on the surface of the ball in the area of most frequent contact with the lane. The diameter of the ball track varies from one bowler to another, ranging from very small (a *spinner*) to intermediate (a *semiroller*) to the full circumference of the ball (a *full roller*) (see Figure 5.4).

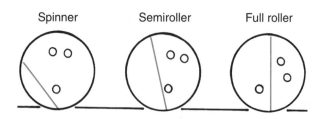

Spinner          Semiroller          Full roller

**Figure 5.4** Range of ball tracks (right-handed bowler).

## Why Are Straight and Hook Balls Important?

A straight ball is valuable for a beginner to learn accuracy and for any bowler who finds the hook ball unreliable on a *difficult lane condition* (an unusual state of friction between the ball and the lane surface). In such a case, the straight ball may be significantly easier to control for strikes and spares than a hook.

A hook ball is the best strike ball because it knocks down, or *carries*, 10 pins more effectively; therefore, it is preferred by professional bowlers. Although the hook ball is more sensitive to variations in lane conditions than the straight ball, the greater striking power of the hook ball compensates for such a disadvantage, particularly on less difficult lane conditions.

The hook ball carries pins better because it has a steeper *angle of attack* into the *pocket* (the desired point of impact for a strike). The angle of attack is formed by two imaginary lines: one drawn straight down the 17th board (1-3 pocket for right-handed bowlers; 1-2 pocket for left-handed bowlers) and the other drawn in line with the direction in which the ball is rolling when it hits the pocket (see Figure 5.5). The straight ball's angle of attack can be no greater than that formed by a line drawn down the 17th board and one from the outer edge of the lane at the foul line to the strike pocket. The hook affords a steeper angle because it rolls into the pocket from the point it begins to hook—the *break point*.

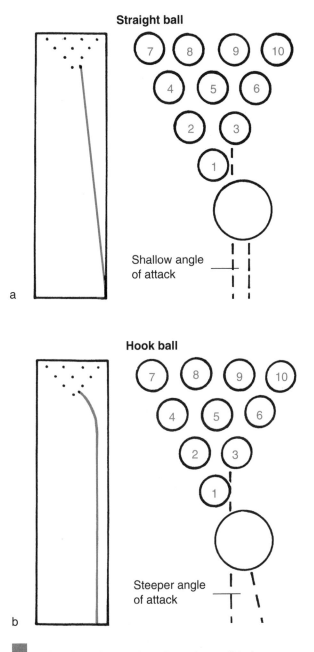

**Figure 5.5** The angles of attack possible for a straight ball and hook ball.

and/or the slicker the pin deck, the greater the potential for deflection of the ball.

Another reason the hook ball has greater carrying power than the straight ball is that it makes pins tilt and spin more. Although a straight ball rolling through a rack of pins imparts some rotation to the pins which it contacts, greater pin action results from a hook ball with a tilted *axis of rotation*. This *axis* is a line passing through the center of the ball and through the center of a plane formed by the ball track (see Figure 5.7). The axis tilt of a bowler's ball

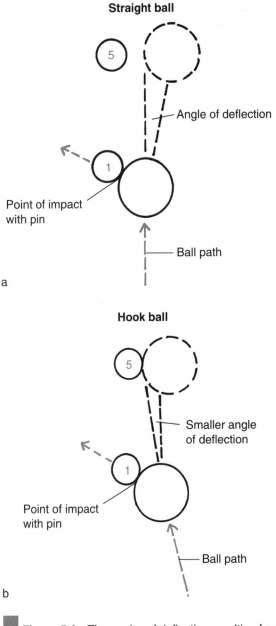

**Figure 5.6** The angles of deflection resulting from a straight ball and a hook ball.

The hook ball's steeper angle of attack lessens the effect of *deflection*—the deviation of the ball path after an off-center impact with a pin—by increasing the chance of the ball to hit the 5 pin, or *kingpin*, which sits directly behind the 1 pin, or *headpin* (see Figures 5.6 and 5.8). The amount of deflection depends on (1) the ball weight (mass), (2) the amount of friction on the *pin deck* (the place where the pins are set up), (3) the resistance of the pins, and (4) the speed (velocity) of the ball. Given the same ball speed and pin resistance, the lighter the ball weight

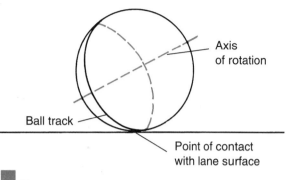

**Figure 5.7** Bowling ball axis of rotation and ball track.

depends on the angle of his or her hand to the lane at the release.

A ball with a tilted axis with respect to the lane actually makes the pins tilt and spin when it contacts them, sending them *careening* through the air. The pin's own axis gyrates; a pin flying in this manner sweeps through a larger area of a plane parallel with the lane, which increases its chance of hitting other pins (see Figure 5.9).

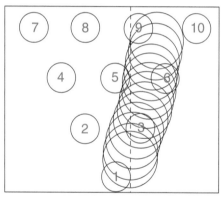

Deflection of straight ball

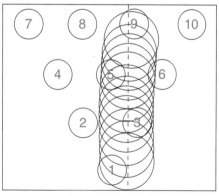

Deflection of hook ball

**Figure 5.8** Deflection path of straight and hook balls rolling through a rack of pins.

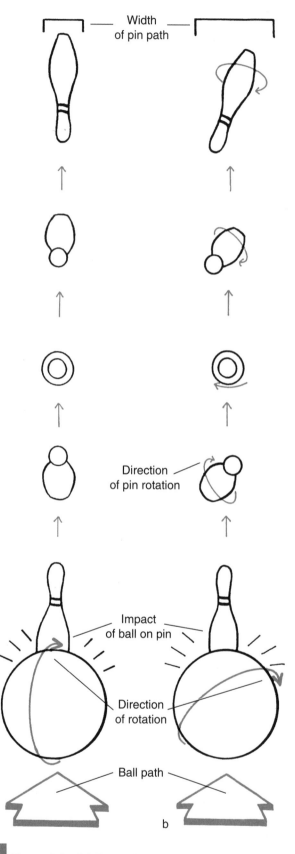

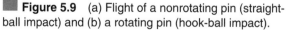

**Figure 5.9** (a) Flight of a nonrotating pin (straight-ball impact) and (b) a rotating pin (hook-ball impact).

## Choosing Between Straight and Hook Balls

Use a hook ball for strikes whenever possible, and use the more reliable straight ball for most spares. On a completely uniform lane condition—a rare situation with equal friction over the entire lane surface—you can make spares with equal efficiency using the hook ball.

To understand the reason for this choice, you should understand a little something about lane conditions. A wooden lane is usually covered with a urethane coating (*lane finish*), which is protected from ball abrasion by a daily application of oil (*lane dressing*) (see Figure 5.10). Ball reaction is remarkably dependent on the amount and location of the dressing on the lane and the state of repair of the lane finish.

If a lane condition is *hooking* (slow, high-friction), *slick* (fast, low-friction), or *spotty* (a mixture of high- and low-friction areas), a hook ball may act unpredictably, with strikes occurring less frequently and splits and multiple-pin *spare leaves* (pins left standing) increasing in frequency. In such a case, switching to a straight ball—playing it safe—would allow better control and consistency. In summary, the hook ball is preferred on well-maintained lane conditions, whereas the straight ball is more reliable on difficult lane conditions.

There are two major reasons why a straight ball may be more reliable on difficult lane conditions. First, in a properly rolled straight ball, lift is applied by the fingers in line with the desired ball path; this action tends to dynamically stabilize the ball in the direction it is rolling.

Second, because the straight-ball delivery requires the hand to stay behind the ball (therefore closer to the body), more of the body's momentum can be transferred to the ball at the release. This gives the ball more forward speed and makes it more resistant to deviation by lane surface irregularities. However, to maximize pin carry, a straight ball must begin to roll soon after touchdown on the lane surface; it should not be skidding, a dynamic that makes the ball easier to deflect upon impact with a pin.

For more information on lane conditions and adjustments to them, see Allen and Ritger (1981), Strickland (1980), and Weber and Alexander (1981).

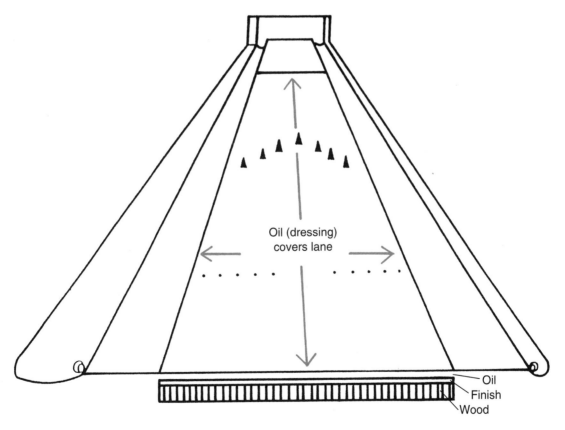

Oil (dressing) covers lane

Oil
Finish
Wood

**Figure 5.10** The lane condition.

# How to Execute a Straight-Ball Delivery

To execute the straight-ball delivery, take a normal setup at your usual location on the approach, using the second arrow visual target assigned in Step 1. Swing and roll the ball with your palm up and your gripping fingers pointed toward 12 o'clock (see Figure 5.11). Keep your elbow *hinge* (the direction in which your elbow bends) perpendicular to your swing (see Figure 5.12). Keep your wrist firm in the 180-

degree, extended position. Use your *supporting fingers* (your index and little fingers) to hold the ball firmly. This action will make your thumb *clear* (leave its hole) more easily. After your thumb has cleared and just before the lifting motion, curl your fingers.

Make a mental picture of squeezing a rubber ball with only your fingers during your release and follow-through. Note that your thumb is straight—not curled (see Figure 5.13). The squeeze will assist you in lifting your ball up and out and onto the lane surface so that it will roll directly in line with the desired ball path.

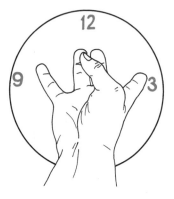

**Figure 5.11** Clock face diagram of the straight-ball hand position.

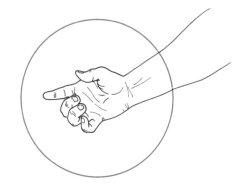
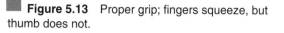

**Figure 5.13** Proper grip; fingers squeeze, but thumb does not.

Keep your fingertips in the 12-o'clock position until you complete your follow-through. Keep your elbow hinge perpendicular to your swing. Maintain the firm wrist (see Figure 5.14).

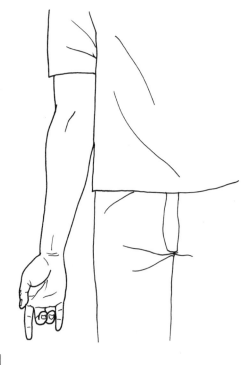

**Figure 5.12** Elbow hinge with fingers in straight-ball position.

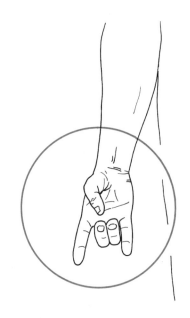

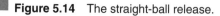
**Figure 5.14** The straight-ball release.

In your final recovery position, hold your fingers at 12 o'clock in the follow-through, with the back of your bowling hand high and presenting itself to the pins. Keep your fingers curled. Your eyes should still be bonded to your target. Pose in this well-balanced position until the ball hits the pins; observe the ball dynamics on the lane.

*Result on the lane*: Your properly executed straight ball should proceed along a path from your hand, over the desired target point (in this case, the second arrow), directly to the desired point of impact with the pins. It should not veer to the outside (back up) or to the inside (hook) (see Figure 5.15).

Your ball should roll "end-over-end" along the target line. It should not be skidding or sliding (see Figure 5.16), and the ball should not track over the grip holes (see Figure 5.17).

## How to Execute A Hook-Ball Delivery

You roll a hook ball by imparting lift in a direction not in line with the ball path, so that the ball will skid farther down the lane. It will begin its roll into the pins from the break point (see Figure 5.18) for a steeper angle of attack.

To execute the hook-ball delivery, take a setup at your usual location on the approach, using the assigned visual target. Swing and roll the ball with your palm and your gripping fingers pointed about 45 degrees to the inside of your swing plane. This will mean a clockface finger position of 10 o'clock for a right-handed bowler (see Figure 5.19), or 2 o'clock for a left-handed bowler. Hold your hand firmly in this position as you swing and deliver your ball. As with the straight ball, keep your elbow hinge perpendicular to your swing throughout your delivery and follow-through (see Figure 5.20). Only your hand—not your elbow hinge—is at the 45-degree angle.

Keep your wrist firm and use your supporting fingers (see Figure 5.21). Curl your fingers as you lift the ball out, onto the lane. The effective hook ball is a predominantly rolling ball, but it does have some spin, or horizontal rotation. However, do not allow your hand, your forearm, or your upper arm to rotate; any spin the hook ball possesses should be

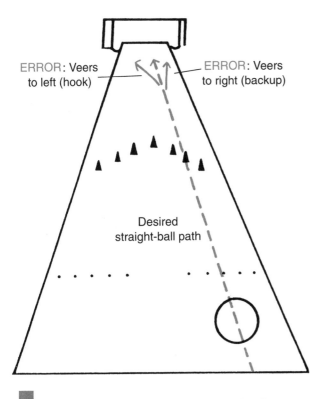

**Figure 5.15** Correct and incorrect paths of straight ball.

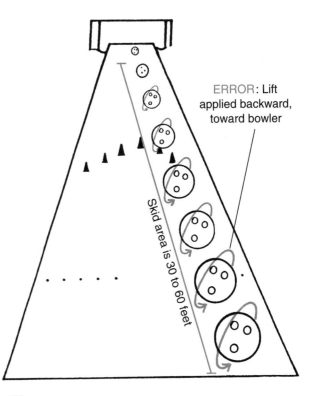

**Figure 5.16** Incorrect—ball is skidding or sliding instead of rolling.

ERROR: Ball track over the grip holes

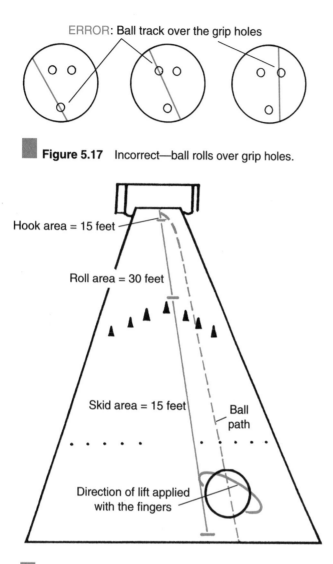

**Figure 5.17** Incorrect—ball rolls over grip holes.

Hook area = 15 feet

Roll area = 30 feet

Skid area = 15 feet

Ball path

Direction of lift applied with the fingers

**Figure 5.18** Hook-ball lift and roll dynamics.

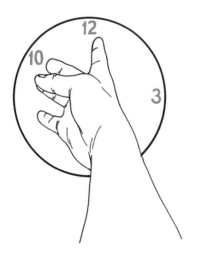

12

10

3

**Figure 5.19** Clock face diagram of the hook-ball hand position.

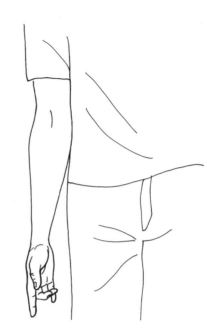

**Figure 5.20** Elbow hinge with fingers in hook-ball position.

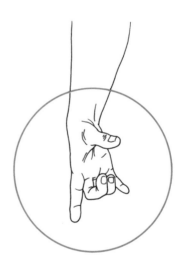

**Figure 5.21** The hook-ball release.

produced only by your lifting fingers held stable in the prescribed position—not by any turning motion of your wrist or arm. Roll your hook ball at exactly the same speed as your straight ball; do not, by any means, speed up or slow down your ball to obtain a hook.

In your final recovery position, keep your curled fingers at a 45-degree angle to the inside position. Keep your eyes bonded to your target. Keep your elbow hinge perpendicular to your swing and your wrist firm. Hold this well-balanced position until the ball makes contact with the pins; observe the ball dynamics on the lane.

*Result on the lane*: Your properly executed hook ball should proceed along a straight path from your hand, over the target point (in this case, the second arrow), and down the lane. At the break point, between approximately two-thirds to three-quarters of the way down the lane, the ball should veer toward the inside of the lane on its way to the desired point of impact with the object pins (see Figure 5.22). Be aware of potential target errors and/or impact misses to either the inside or the outside (see Figure 5.23).

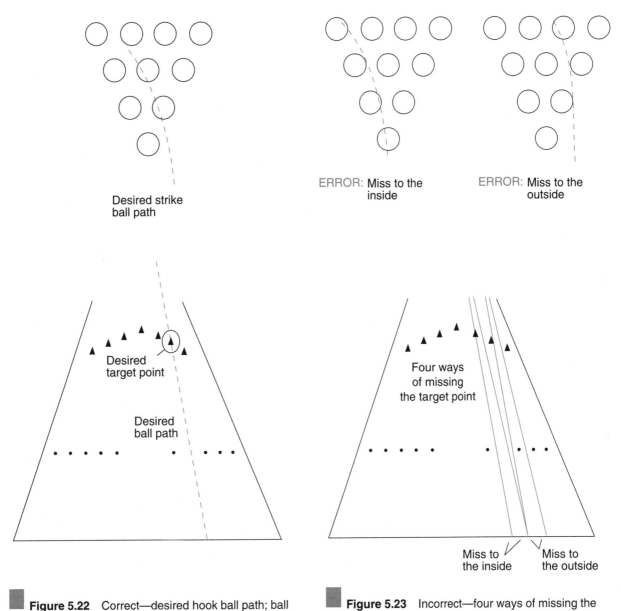

**Figure 5.22**  Correct—desired hook ball path; ball hits target point.

**Figure 5.23**  Incorrect—four ways of missing the target point.

## BALL DYNAMICS SUCCESS STOPPERS

When properly executed, both your straight and hook ball should proceed along a path from the hand, over the visual target. Your hook ball should veer toward the inside of the lane on its way to the desired point of impact with the pins. You can increase your consistency if you learn how to recognize common errors in ball dynamics.

| Error | Correction |
| --- | --- |
| **Straight Ball** | |
| 1. Ball veers off to one side of the lane instead of going straight along the desired path. | 1. Make sure to hold your fingers at 12 o'clock; keep your wrist firm and your elbow hinge locked perpendicular to your swing plane. |
| 2. Ball seems to be skidding or sliding instead of rolling. | 2. Keep your wrist firm and push into your finish. Feel your shoulder push, your elbow lock, your thumb clear, and your fingers lift the ball up and onto the lane surface. Your thumb may be *hanging* in the thumbhole, so have a trained person check your ball fit. |
| 3. If you hear a "thump, thump," the ball is rolling over the grip holes. | 3. Check and correct your finger position, your wrist firmness, and the ball fit. Keep your elbow locked. Do not rotate your wrist at the point of release. Keep your thumb straight inside the hole. |
| **Hook Ball** | |
| 1. Ball misses either the target point, the desired point of impact with the pins, or both. | 1. Make sure you do not hold your fingers too far toward the inside (8 or 9 o'clock for a right-handed bowler, 3 or 4 o'clock for a left-hander). This would allow your arm to move too far away from the body, making the ball touch down too far to the outside. Have a trained observer check your delivery. |
| 2. Ball hooks too little, or too much, or inconsistently. | 2. Keep your wrist firm and your fingers in the proper position. Make sure that you are rolling the ball at normal speed (and at the same speed each time) and that you feel good leverage at the release. Your thumb may be hanging, so have a trained person check your ball fit. |
| 3. Ball rolls over the grip holes. | 3. Check and correct your finger position, your wrist firmness, and the ball fit. Keep your elbow locked. Do not rotate your wrist to the inside or the outside at the release. Keep your thumb straight in the hole. |

## BALL DYNAMICS

# DRILLS

*Courtesy Tip*: Always check for clearance on either side so that you do not annoy others or injure yourself or anyone around you.

### 1. Power Push Straight-Ball Finish

Build strength into your straight-ball release! Because the straight-ball hand position places your lifting fingers closer to your sliding foot, you can use this drill to learn the feel of increasingly greater leverage as you attain better timing between your swing and your slide. Do not be concerned with where your ball hits the pins.

Assume a normal setup and take a "One-Step Delivery" (as necessary, review Step 4, Drill 2). Hold your hand in the straight-ball position throughout. Stare at your visual target and focus your attention on the characteristics listed in the Success Check, below. You should feel more pressure on your lifting fingers (you have your "fingers in the shot") and feel your bowling shoulder support your straight bowling arm (you have your "shoulder in the shot").

**Success Goal** = 3 one-step deliveries per Success Check (18 total deliveries) ___

### ✔ Success Check
- Normal setup ___
- Fingers at 12 o'clock ___
- Power push delivery ___
- Firm wrist at release ___
- Push from shoulder ___
- Squeeze with fingers ___

### To Increase Difficulty
- Try to "line up" and hit the target and the pocket with your straight ball. When your ball hits the second arrow, notice where it contacts the pins and move your feet, 2 boards at a time, in the same direction as the ball that missed the pocket until your ball is hitting the pocket. Try to hit the pocket as many times in a row as you can. Do not shoot spares.

### To Decrease Difficulty
- Start with no ball or a lighter-weight ball.

## 2. Full Straight-Ball Delivery

Get the feel of a full straight-ball delivery. Assume your normal setup position, adjust your fingers to point toward 12 o'clock, and take a flowing, well-executed four-step delivery, rolling a straight ball over your target (second arrow). Every time you return from the foul line, ask yourself whether you felt that your fingers and your shoulder were in your shot. If you did not, you lost leverage at some stage in your delivery.

**Success Goal** = 3 straight-ball deliveries per Success Check (18 total straight-ball deliveries) ___

### Success Check
- Fingers at 12 o'clock ___
- Normal setup and delivery ___
- Firm wrist at release ___
- Push with shoulder ___
- Stable balance arm ___
- Squeeze with fingers after thumb clears ___

### To Increase Difficulty
- Increase the number of deliveries; stop when tired or when you begin to experience a loss of coordination.
- Bowl (and score) a game using only straight-ball deliveries.

### To Decrease Difficulty
- Use no ball and walk through each portion slowly.
- Use a lighter-weight ball.

## 3. Power Push Hook-Ball Finish

Build strength into your hook-ball release! Assume a normal setup and take the "One-Step Delivery" (as necessary, review Step 4, Drill 2). Hold your hand in the hook-ball position throughout. Align your bowling elbow hinge perpendicular to your intended swing plane, then move your fingers 45 degrees to the inside of the 12 o'clock position; keep your wrist firm and straight. It is absolutely vital to your consistency that your elbow hinge remains perfectly perpendicular to your swing, even though your fingers are not!

Focus your attention on the leverage linkage among your body segments. If your swing and slide are in time with one another, you should feel that your lifting fingers and your bowling shoulder are in the shot during your hook-ball release.

**Success Goal** = 3 hook-ball deliveries per Success Check (21 total hook-ball deliveries) ___

### Success Check
- Normal setup ___
- Fingers at 10 o'clock (2 o'clock for left-hander) ___
- Power push delivery ___
- Firm wrist at release ___
- Push from shoulder ___
- Squeeze with fingers after thumb clears ___
- Release with fingers at 10 o'clock (2 o'clock for left-hander) ___

### To Increase Difficulty
- Try to "line up" and hit the target and the pocket with your hook ball. When your ball hits the second arrow, notice where it contacts the pins and move your feet, 2 boards at a time, in the same direction that the ball missed the pocket until your ball is hitting the pocket. Try to hit the pocket as many times in a row as you can. Do not shoot spares.

### To Decrease Difficulty
- Start with no ball or a lighter-weight ball.

## 4. Full Hook-Ball Delivery

Get the feel of a full hook-ball delivery. Assume your normal setup position and take a flowing, well-executed four-step delivery, rolling a hook ball toward your target (second arrow). Every time you return from the foul line, ask yourself whether you felt that your fingers and shoulder were in your shot. If you did not, look for lost leverage at some stage in your delivery (i.e., you may have broken your wrist back, yielding to the additional force instead of increasing wrist firmness by pushing with your supporting fingers).

**Success Goal** = 3 hook-ball deliveries per Success Check (21 total hook-ball deliveries) ___

**Success Check**
- Fingers at 10 o'clock (2 o'clock for left-hander) ___
- Normal setup and delivery ___
- Firm wrist at release ___
- Push from shoulder ___
- Stable balance arm ___
- Squeeze with fingers after thumb clears ___
- Release with fingers at 10 o'clock (2 o'clock for left-hander) ___

**To Increase Difficulty**
- Increase the number of deliveries; stop when tired or when you begin to experience a loss of coordination.
- Bowl (and score) a game using only hook-ball deliveries.

**To Decrease Difficulty**
- Use no ball and walk through each portion slowly.
- Use a lighter-weight ball.

## BALL DYNAMICS SUCCESS SUMMARY

You now understand how ball dynamics can affect the skidding and rolling motions of a bowling ball as it proceeds down the lane toward the pins. You should be able to make your ball roll consistently down the lane, whether using a straight or a hook release. With frequent practice, your fingers, hand, and wrist will grow stronger, and your ball dynamics will become more effective. Practice smart!

# STEP 6

## STRIKE TARGETING: KNOCKING THEM ALL DOWN

One of the most exciting scenes in bowling is the strike. Whether "solid," with the pins being pushed off the lane all at once, or "mixing," with the pins spinning and twisting side to side, no one can deny how pleasing a strike is to bowler and spectator alike. The crashing sound of pins keeps people coming back again and again.

You get strikes—knocking all the pins down with the first ball—by making accurate, well-executed shots, rolling a straight or hook ball, toward intelligently selected targets on the lane. A *target* is some mark—a dark spot in a board, a crack between boards, an arrow, or a dot at which you aim. A *system* is an ordered group of principles, a plan, or a method by which to accomplish something. By consistent use of a *targeting system*, you can maximize your chances for a strike before you roll your ball.

In this step you'll learn a *target-line system*, which minimizes interference with your swing or your *gait* (walking pattern) to the foul line. First, straight-ball strike targeting is presented, because its dynamics limit variability of results at the pins and provide you with more clear-cut feedback on the success of your efforts. Then you will learn hook-ball strike targeting, taking into account the size of your hook when selecting your target line. You will be able to execute your shot comfortably and confidently, using the feel of your shot as feedback to keep yourself executing correctly.

## Why Is Strike Targeting Important?

First of all, a targeting system is important because it allows you to be more accurate. Such a system incorporates *visual targets* (eye *fixation points*) close to you on the lane. It is more difficult to consistently hit a desired point of pin impact 60 feet from the foul line using only the pins as a visual target. For this reason, bowlers seriously desiring higher scores usually develop the use of closer targets.

Second, proper use of a targeting system can help you maintain superior execution from shot to shot. If the path you walk bears the proper parallel relationship with your desired ball path, you will be able to swing your ball and walk to the foul line comfortably. If the path does not, you may unconsciously try to force your ball to hit a target for which your body is not aligned, thereby corrupting your swing.

A third important point is that if you roll a hook, a targeting system will build control and confidence by helping you *find your line* (locate the best path for your ball to follow), as soon as possible after you start to bowl. If you do not take this precaution, you may assume that the reason for an unexpected ball reaction is poor execution, which is often not the case. Such an assumption may start a chain of poorly chosen compensations that can destroy your feel for proper execution and, ultimately, your confidence.

Finally, systematic targeting makes you more responsive to changing lane conditions. Even if you find your line quickly and execute well, the lane condition changes as time passes, requiring you to move your target line for your shots to stay in the pocket. The rule of thumb is this: "Get in time, get on line, get in the groove, and stay in the groove."

## Aiming Methods

Four different *alignment*, or aiming, methods are commonly described in bowling texts. These are pin bowling; spot bowling; line bowling; and target-line, or parallel-line, bowling.

*Pin bowling* is not an effective way to aim at all. It involves nothing more than standing anywhere on the approach and rolling the ball in the general direction of the rack of pins.

*Spot bowling,* bowling at a spot (any visual target) on the lane surface, provides greater accuracy than pin bowling because the chosen spot is closer. Because no instruction is usually given concerning a setup location for a given spot, the only definite reference point is the spot itself. Therefore, a bowler is left unguided in picking a place to stand on the approach, increasing the likelihood that a poor choice of a setup location may be made for a given target. The choice may or may not promote a well-coordinated delivery.

*Line bowling* has been given many different descriptions in bowling texts. None of these descriptions has been adequate, because they refer to as many as five points of reference for a ball path, without regard to how these points are to be used as visual targets in the setup and during movement. Further, no advice has been given as to where to stand in relation to a given ball path.

*Target-line (parallel-line) bowling* is the only true targeting system because it describes a logical relationship between where to look and where to stand during the setup and delivery. You'll use this system to select a setup location that makes your *approach line* (the path you walk to the foul line) parallel with your *target line* (the desired ball path). In this way, you align your swing plane over your target line so that you can execute your delivery comfortably and project your ball over two necessary points—one at the foul line and one a little farther down the lane at the arrows (see Figure 6.1).

## How to Execute Strike Targeting

Strike targeting follows a systematic series of actions, which have been numbered (1 through 10) on the following pages. The first two actions need to be performed only until you have committed the details to memory. Notice that the remaining actions (3 through 10) are part of a target-line adjustment cycle. Use this cycle often to make changes in your hook-ball

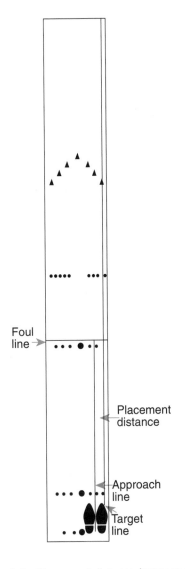

**Figure 6.1** Placement distance between target line and approach line.

path in response to changing lane conditions. Follow these actions in order.

*1. **Learn the Lane Targets.*** The target-line system utilizes certain markers placed on the lane surface. The characteristic arrows and dots are collectively called *Rangefinders.* (They were developed by the Brunswick Corporation and are illustrated in Figure 6.2, a and b.)

Regardless of which hand you bowl with, always try to refer to approach and lane boards by number. There are 39 boards in a lane, each slightly over 1 inch wide. Identify these boards by counting them from the *outside* (your swingside) channel in the direction of the *inside* (your balance-side) channel. The first of the succeeding diagrams illustrates the numbering system to be used by a right-handed bowler;

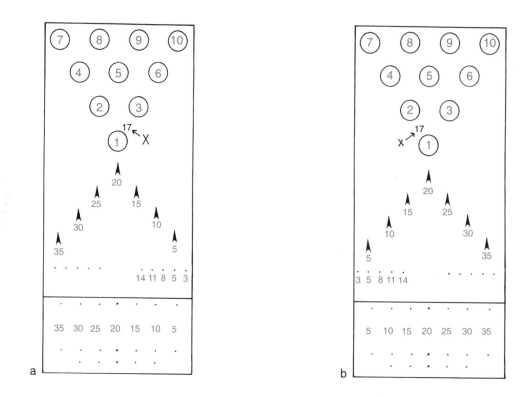

**Figure 6.2** Board numbering system (a) for a right-handed bowler, and (b) for a left-handed bowler.

the second diagram illustrates the numbering system to be used by a left-hander. If you are left-handed, count boards from your left to your right; if right-handed, count boards from your right to your left.

The *Rangefinder* arrows are placed on every fifth board. Beginning from your outside channel, the first arrow has been placed on board number 5, the second on board number 10, the third on board number 15, and so on; the last arrow is on board number 35. The dots at the foul line are placed on the same board numbers as the arrows, but the small dots 6 feet from the foul line are on board numbers 3, 5, 8, 11, and 14. The approach dots 12 and 15 feet before the foul line, however, are usually placed only on boards 10, 15, 20 (the largest, center dot), 25, and 30. In some establishments, there are two additional dots, one on 5 and the other on 35.

Here are some examples of arrow and dot relationships:

- The 2nd arrow is outside the 3rd.
- The 2nd arrow is placed on the 10th board from the outside.
- The headpin is centered on board number 20.
- The center arrow is inside with respect to the swingside channel.
- The 1st arrow is on the 5th board.

- The 4th arrow is inside with respect to the 3rd arrow.
- The 5th arrow is located on board number 25.

*2. Determine Your Placement Distance.* Before you begin learning how to use targets, you must determine the size of your *placement distance* (PD). This measure is the distance in boards between your sliding foot (generally its inside edge) and the point of contact of your ball at or near the foul line (see Figure 6.3).

The PD also reflects the horizontal distance between your body's center of gravity and the center of your ball. It is important for you to know this distance so you can determine the appropriate setup location for a particular target line. Large persons with broad shoulders have large placement distances; smaller persons exhibit smaller placement distances. The average PD range is 6 to 8 boards. A placement distance will remain constant for the lifetime of any particular bowler whose weight is consistent. Drill 2 within this step will help you determine your own PD.

*3. Choose a Target Point.* The place where you desire your ball to roll by the arrows is your target point. Let's assume that this target point is your visual target. For now, look at the second arrow from

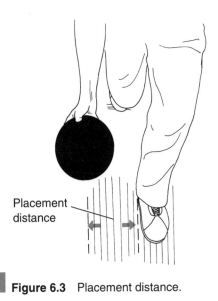

**Figure 6.3** Placement distance.

the outside, located on the 10th board (the 10th from the outside channel).

**4. Choose Your Ball's Touchdown Point.** The point you choose reflects the angle at which you desire to roll your ball over your target point.

*Straight Ball:* You are temporarily assigned the 8 board as the point at which your ball will touch down, the *touchdown point.* Therefore, your straight-ball target line will be "8 to 10," referring to your two reference points.

*Hook Ball:* You need to make some adjustments. To straight-ball bowlers, lane conditions are similar from lane to lane. However, to hook-ball bowlers, each lane has a distinct *hook power,* or tendency for a ball to hook. Therefore, you must roll one or more balls to see how much your ball hooks before you can know where your ball should touch down to strike while you use a given target point. For now, you are assigned a *test target line* of 10 to 10. You will be rolling your test balls straight down the 10th board from the outside channel, "down ten," and watching how your ball "reacts." Later, you will get a chance to sharpen your skills at adjusting your target line (at *playing lanes*) with the hook ball.

**5. Project an Imaginary Extension.** Visualize an extension of your target line back to the area of the approach at which you take your setup.

*Straight Ball:* Because you stand about the same distance from the foul line as the second arrow is from the foul line, you may assume that the imaginary target-line extension crosses your setup area at about the 6th board (10 – 8 = 2, 8 – 2 = 6) (see Figure 6.4).

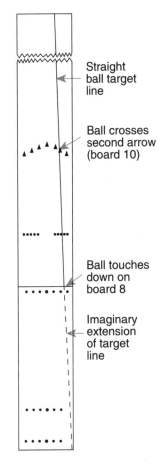

**Figure 6.4** Imaginary extension of straight-ball target line.

*Hook Ball:* Since your test target line is 10 to 10, your extended target line would cross your setup area at board 10 (see Figure 6.5).

**6. Take Your Setup at the Appropriate Location With Respect to Your Target Line.** Position both feet so that they are parallel with each other and with your target line.

*Straight Ball:* To find the setup point for the inside of your sliding foot sole, simply add your placement distance to the number 6. Let's assume that your placement distance is 7; therefore, 6 + 7 gives you a setup location of the 13th board.

When you deliver a straight ball, your intended approach line now begins on board 13 at your setup location and ends on board 15 at the foul line. Place the edge of your sliding foot on the edge of board 13 so that the board is completely visible to the arch side of your foot.

*Hook Ball:* For your test target line of 10 to 10, adding a hypothetical placement distance (PD) of 7 boards gives you a setup location of 17. Your intended

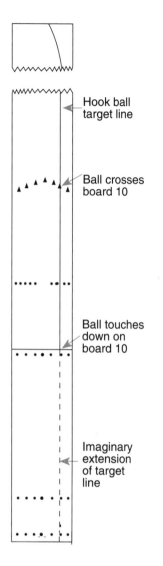

**Figure 6.5** Imaginary extension of hook-ball target line.

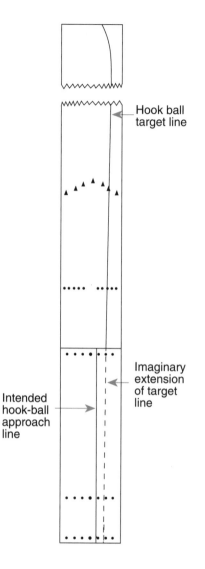

**Figure 6.6** Intended hook-ball approach line.

approach line begins on board 17 at your setup location, and ends on board 17 at the foul line. Place the edge of your sliding foot on the edge of board 17 so that the board is completely visible to the arch side of your foot (see Figure 6.6).

**7. *Fix Your Eyes on Your Visual Target.*** Keeping your eyes fixed on a well-defined visual target is valuable in stabilizing your head, neck, and back to keep them from moving during your delivery (see Figure 6.7). Further, the act of fixing your gaze on a visual target draws your body toward the target during your approach. The visual target is a "lure." Your visual target may not be the same as your target point; you may have to look at a visual target to the inside or outside of the target point in order to roll your ball over the target point itself.

**8. *Execute Your Shot Properly.*** Get into the habit of evaluating the quality of your execution before you ask, "What did my ball do?"

**9. *Analyze Your Shot.*** Make sure that you watch your ball proceed down the lane, observing where your ball passed the arrows and where it contacted the pins. Also, look down at your sliding foot to see on what board your slide stopped. Your straight ball should proceed along a path from your hand, over the target point, and straight to the strike pocket at the 17th board. Figure 6.8 shows the desired straight-ball path. Your hook ball should proceed straight along a path from your hand, over your target point, to the break point. From the break point, the ball should move toward the strike pocket at the 17th board. Figure 6.9 shows the desired hook-ball path.

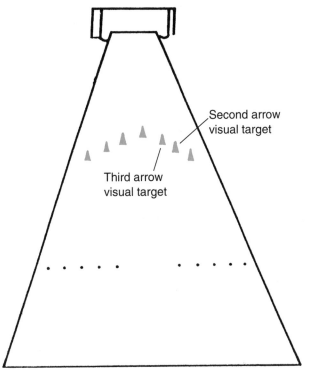

**Figure 6.7** Common visual targets for right-handed bowlers.

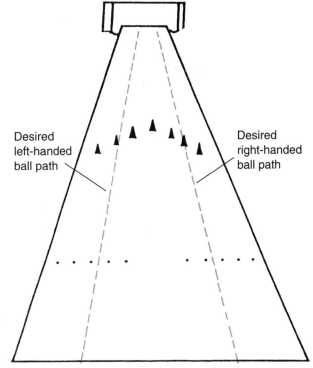

**Figure 6.8** Desired straight ball path.

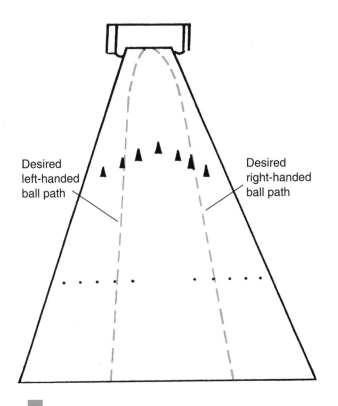

**Figure 6.9** Desired hook ball path.

For both straight and hook balls, there are two common alignment errors. In both errors, your ball hits one target, but misses the other. These misses may be to the inside or to the outside (see Figure 6.10).

***10. Correct Your Shot Appropriately.*** Take the following courses of action when making either straight- or hook-ball adjustments:

- If you executed properly, if your ball passed over the correct board at the arrows, and if it went on to contact the pins at the strike pocket (at the 17th board from the outside channel), roll another properly executed shot along the same target line.
- If you did not execute properly, regardless of whether your ball passed over the correct board at the arrows or contacted the pins at the strike pocket, do not make any adjustments to your target line until you have corrected your execution.
- If you executed properly and your ball passed over the correct board at the arrows, but did not contact the pins at the strike pocket, verify the correctness of and make adjustments to your target line by repeating actions 4 through

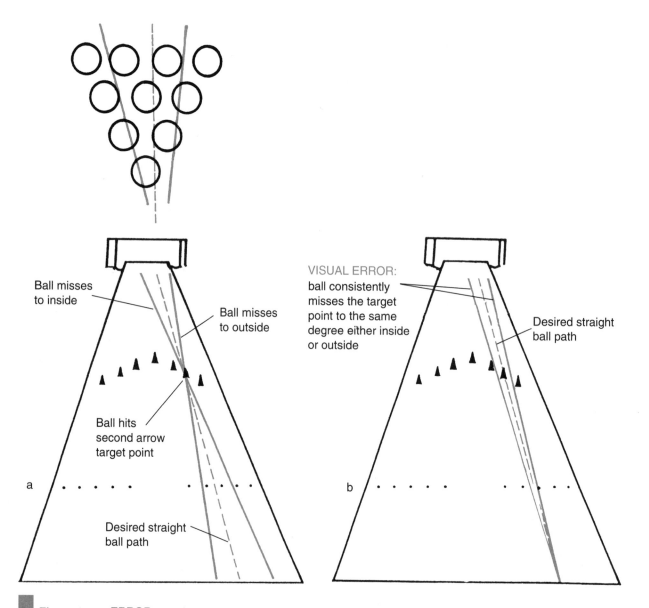

**Figure 6.10** ERROR: Two ways to miss the strike pocket: (a) ball misses touchdown point and (b) ball misses arrow target.

9 and using the following "3-0-1-2 System." Be sure that you saw where your ball rolled; the rule is, "If you cannot remember where your ball rolled, you did not see it!"

## The 3-0-1-2 System

This system is very reliable and is based on all adjustments to the target line pivoting on a single visual target. In other words, if you wanted to change the angle of your ball's path, you would keep the visual target constant.

The four components to the 3-0-1-2 system are expressed in terms of the "number of boards of change" from a previous target line. These are the location of ball impact at the pins (the "3"), the location of the visual target (the "0"), the point at which the ball touches down (the "1"), and the relative location of the setup (the "2"). You really need to be concerned only with the location of ball impact (the "3") and where you stand (the "2").

The rule of the 3-0-1-2 system is, "For every 3 boards of desired change in the location of impact of the ball with the pins, move your setup location at the back of the approach by 2 boards in the *opposite* direction.

Keep your visual target at the same location. This adjustment will result in a 1-board change in the location of the ball's touchdown point at the foul line."

Let's look at an example: You are a right-handed bowler who rolled your ball perfectly along your chosen 10-to-10 target line, but it hit the 4-pin slightly to the left of center. How would you move, using the 3-0-1-2 system, so that your next ball would (theoretically) hit directly in the strike pocket?

**Solution:**

1. Determine near which numbered board the ball contacted the pins. The 4 pin is centered on board 30, but the off-center hit may have been on board 32.
2. Subtract the point of pocket impact (board 17) from the actual point of impact (board 32). The amount of error is 32 – 17 = 15 boards to the left.
3. Apply the 3-0-1-2 rule, divide 15 by 3 to yield 5. Then multiply 5 by 2 to yield 10—the number of boards you should move your setup to the left.
4. Test the adjustment. Stand 10 boards further to the inside (the left for a right-handed bowler) and use the same visual target as before. If you execute properly and roll your ball over the same target point at the level of the arrows, your ball should hit the pocket. If your ball does not hit the pocket, determine the amount of error and move your setup location again, using the 3-0-1-2 system.

Effective strike targeting using the target-line system is nothing more than becoming skilled at carrying out the mental checklist illustrated in Figure 6.11 (p. 81). For more information on strike targeting, see Allen and Ritger (1981).

## STRIKE-TARGETING SUCCESS STOPPERS

You can increase the consistency with which you roll your ball into the strike pocket if you learn how to recognize errors in strike targeting. Some common errors and suggestions on how to correct them follow.

| Error | Correction |
|---|---|
| **Straight Ball** | |
| 1. Ball misses target to the inside and hits too *high* on the headpin, or it completely misses the headpin to the inside. | 1. Make sure you execute properly and your swing is in line with your shoulder and the target. Also, make sure you do not look to the inside of the target. |
| 2. Ball misses target to the outside and hits too *lightly* on the headpin, or it completely misses the headpin to the outside. | 2. Make sure you execute properly and your swing is in line with your shoulder and the target. Also, make sure you do not look to the outside of the target. |
| 3. Ball consistently hits the target but misses the desired point of impact at the pins to the same degree each time. | 3. Make sure you execute properly and your swing is in line with your shoulder and the target. If these check out OK, use the 3-0-1-2 system to adjust your setup location. |

| Error | Correction |
|---|---|
| ***Straight Ball (continued)*** | |
| 4. Ball consistently misses target to the same degree. | 4. Make sure you execute properly and your swing is in line with your shoulder and the target.<br><br>If the ball is still missing the target, you may have a visual error for which you must compensate. Move your gaze in the direction opposite your error until your ball is consistently rolling over your chosen target point. (Note: You may always have to look at a visual target that is to one side of your intended target point to compensate for a vision problem. Experimentation is often necessary.) |
| 5. Ball consistently hits target and the strike pocket but does not make a strike. | 5. Make sure you execute properly, your wrist is firm, and your swing is in line with your shoulder and the target. Make half-board adjustments to your setup location until your ball is hitting the pocket in the proper way to carry the pins. Always remember the exact location to which you move your feet, and do not move so far that your ball begins to miss the pocket. |
| ***Hook Ball*** | |
| 1. Ball hits target point but misses the strike pocket to the inside, hitting the headpin too full (too high) or missing it altogether on the inside. | 1. Try again with proper execution and the correct visual target. If the second attempt does not work, use the 3-0-1-2 system to adjust your setup location to the inside. |
| 2. Ball hits target point but misses the strike pocket to the outside, hitting the headpin too lightly or missing it altogether. | 2. Try again with proper execution and the correct visual target. If the second attempt does not work, use the 3-0-1-2 system to adjust your setup location to the outside. |
| 3. Ball consistently misses target point. | 3. Make sure you are executing properly and you are using the proper visual target. If the ball is still missing the target, you may have a visual error for which you must compensate. See Straight Ball, Correction #4. |
| 4. Ball consistently hits target and the strike pocket but does not strike consistently. | 4. Make sure you execute properly and your swing is in line with your shoulder and the target. Make slight adjustments in your finger position. For example, change from the 45-degree to a 30- or 60-degree position, to create a different ball reaction. You may have to use the 3-0-1-2 system to move your setup location in response to the different amount of hook. If your hook is bigger, you will have to move your feet to the inside; if smaller, you will have to move your feet outside. |

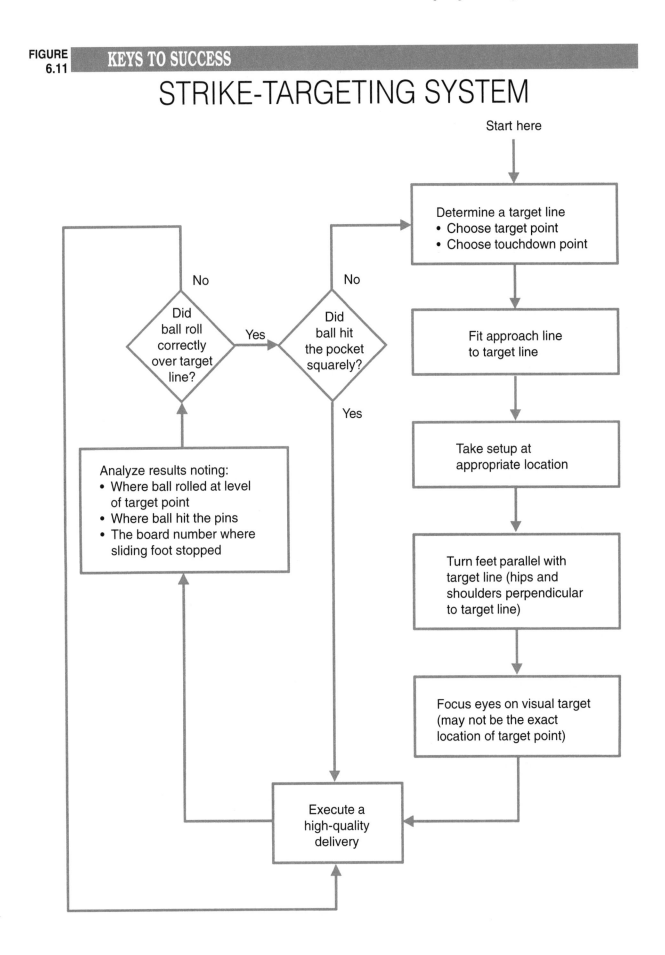

**FIGURE 6.11**

## KEYS TO SUCCESS

# STRIKE-TARGETING SYSTEM

# DRILLS

## *1. Targeting Quiz*

Learn the various targeting aids on the approach and lane. Study the figures that show the location of the pins, dots, and arrows. In addition, study the following figure, which shows the lengths of bowling lane segments. When you feel ready, close the book and answer the following questions. Score yourself, comparing your answers with those at the end of this drill.

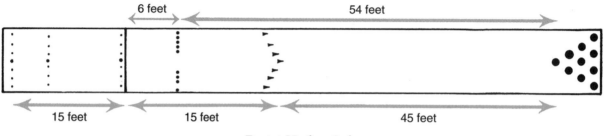

6 feet        54 feet

15 feet        15 feet        45 feet

**Target Marker Quiz**

a. Name, in the following order, the board numbers upon which are set the following pins (10 responses):

1 pin, 7 pin, 10 pin, 5 pin, 8 pin, 9 pin, 2 pin, 3 pin, 4 pin, and 6 pin

b. Name the board numbers upon which are placed the target arrows, from the outside to the inside (7 responses).

c. Name the board numbers upon which are placed the dots at the foul line, from the outside to the inside (7 responses).

d. How far are the two sets of approach dots from the foul line (2 responses)?

e. How far is the foul line from the headpin? The arrows from the foul line? The arrows from the headpin? The small set of lane dots from the foul line? (4 responses; all may be approximate.)

f. Name the board numbers upon which lie the small set of lane dots, from the outside to the inside (5 responses).

 **Success Goal** = 35 out of 35 correct answers ___

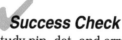 **Success Check**
• Study pin, dot, and arrow lane diagrams ___
• Answer questions ___

### *To Increase Difficulty*
• Using no notes, draw a diagram of the lane and approach dots and the lane arrows.
• Label each with the appropriate board number.

### *To Decrease Difficulty*
• Look at the diagrams while you take the quiz.
• Use partner prompting.

**Answer Key to Target Marker Quiz**

a. Right-handed: 20, 35, 5, 20, 25, 15, 25, 15, 30, 10
Left-handed: 20, 5, 35, 20, 15, 25, 15, 25, 10, 30
(Answers b. through f. apply to both right- and left-handed bowlers.)

b. 5, 10, 15, 20, 25, 30, 35

c. 5, 10, 15, 20, 25, 30, 35

d. 12 feet and 15 feet

e. 60 feet, 15 feet, 45 feet, 6 feet

f. 3, 5, 8, 11, 14

## 2. Placement Distance Determination

Determine your personal placement distance (PD), the distance between your sliding foot and the location where you ball touches down during the release. It is usually necessary to determine your PD only once. However, you may need to repeat the determination if your weight fluctuates greatly.

Take a "sitting tall" finish position with your ball dangling to your swingside. Make sure that your balance arm is correctly positioned and your shoulders are level with the approach. "Sit down" even more, so that your ball touches the approach; keep your back upright and keep your swingside leg behind you so that you must balance on your sliding foot, keeping it directly under your center of gravity.

Have a partner use a ruler to measure the distance between the inner edge of your sliding foot and the point of contact of your ball. Make five measurements in inches, recording them in the Success Goal Section. Take the average as your PD and translate inches to boards by dividing the PD in inches by 1.1 (110%).

Use the PD in boards in all of your subsequent bowling alignment procedures outlined in this book, as well as for all of your future bowling activities.

**Success Goal** = Fill out the following chart to determine personal PD in boards after 5 measurements ___

**Success Check**
• Take "sitting tall" finish position ___
• Measure distance between ball and foot ___
• Translate inches into boards ___

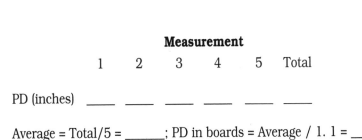

| | **Measurement** | | | | | |
| | 1 | 2 | 3 | 4 | 5 | Total |
| PD (inches) | ___ | ___ | ___ | ___ | ___ | ___ |

Average = Total/5 = _____; PD in boards = Average / 1. 1 = _____

## 3. Straight-Ball Strike Targeting

How accurate is your straight ball? It is now time for you to roll a trial game consisting of 10 scored first-ball deliveries. You will use a straight ball and a target line of 8 to 10.

Your partner will use a scoresheet to record execution information, but not score pinfall or second-ball attempts. After your game has begun, do not talk to your partner except as you will be directed. Prepare your scoresheet following the example of Sample Scoresheet 1.

**Sample Scoresheet 1**

| NAME          HDCP | 1 | 2 | 3 | 4 | 5 | 6 | 7 | 8 | 9 | 10 |
|---|---|---|---|---|---|---|---|---|---|---|
| 1 *Setup location* | | | | | | | | | | |
| 2 *Slide location* | | | | | | | | | | |
| 3 *Target area board* | | | | | | | | | | |
| 4 *Impact board* | | | | | | | | | | |

Take your setup on the same board every time; tell your partner what this board number is before you start, so that it can be entered in all 10 frames of the first game line as the "setup location." After each delivery, look down at your sliding toe, noting the number of the first board that is completely visible just to the inside of your sliding foot. Tell your partner this board number so that it can be recorded as "slide location" in the proper frame of the second game line.

Your partner must watch your ball's reaction—not your form—to gather the rest of the information. Therefore, while you are in your setup, your partner should begin to gaze at the second arrow, your intended target. As your ball rolls down the lane, your partner should note and record in the appropriate frames of your prepared scoresheet the board number over which the ball rolled at the arrows (the *target area board*) and the board number over which the ball rolled when it hit the pins (the *impact board*). Both board numbers should be immediately recorded in the appropriate frames of your scoresheet.

Your partner should give you a check mark (point) for each time an entry matches the ideal (not including setup location). The ideals for the entries should be: Slide location = board 8 + your PD; Target area = board 10; Impact board = board 17. (You may not strike, but hitting the 17th board earns a check mark!)

**Success Goal** = Complete 3 trial games and fill out the following chart from your scoresheet; a perfect score of total points is 90 ___

**Success Check**
- Normal setup at correct location ___
- Normal straight-ball delivery ___
- Second-arrow target ___
- Bowl as consistently as you can ___

|  | Trial game | | |
|---|---|---|---|
| Characteristic | 1 | 2 | 3 |
| Slide location (8 + PD) | ___ | ___ | ___ |
| Target area (10) | ___ | ___ | ___ |
| Impact board (17) | ___ | ___ | ___ |
| *Total points* | ___ | ___ | ___ |

**To Increase Difficulty**
- Score 1 point only if you strike on the 17th board.

**To Decrease Difficulty**
- Bowl only 2 games.
- Score 1 point if you hit the headpin.

## Performance Evaluation

When you have finished, discuss your performance with your partner. Use the following criteria.

a. If the numbers listed in the "slide location" row seem to be consistent—not varying more than one board—you are probably executing your delivery well.

b. If the numbers listed in the "target area" row consistently read "10," congratulations! If they do not, review the "Detecting Straight-Ball Strike-Targeting Errors" section earlier in this Step.

c. If the numbers listed in the "impact point" row consistently read "17," congratulations! If not, check your execution and use the 3-0-1-2 system to correct your target line.

### 4. Hook-Ball Strike Targeting

Now use the targeting system to align your body for striking with your hook ball. Always remember that you must walk parallel with your target line for consistency in hitting the strike pocket. Disregard the fact that you may be walking at an angle to the foul line (away from the pocket) when rolling your hook ball.

Bowl a trial game consisting of 10 first balls. Your partner will act as observer to tell you whether you actually roll your ball over your attempted target line. Take a warm-up first, rolling your ball along a 10-to-10 target line to develop proper execution. Your partner will use two game lines on a scoresheet to record execution information, but not pinfall or second-ball attempts. Prepare a scoresheet, using Sample Scoresheet 2 as a model.

**Sample Scoresheet 2**

| NAME          HDCP | 1 | 2 | 3 | 4 | 5 | 6 | 7 | 8 | 9 | 10 |
|---|---|---|---|---|---|---|---|---|---|---|
| 1 *Target line* | 10 / 10 | | | | | | | | | |
| 2 *Impact point* | | | | | | | | | | |

*Finding a Line:* Before you roll your first ball of each frame in game one, declare your intended target line so your observer can record it and give you feedback with respect to your accuracy. After each of your first-ball attempts, your observer should indicate "yes" if you hit the target line, or "no" if you did not. You should also analyze how your delivery felt; be honest with yourself!

*Note:* You may have to attempt the first ball of each frame more than once to hit the designated target line (moving your setup location using the 3-0-1-2 system) and to make sure that you executed properly before your partner can make any entry in a game line.

After your successful attempt, your partner should enter, in the appropriate frame of the second game line, the board number where your ball rolled as it hit the pins. Then your partner records, in the next frame of the first game line, the target line that you will next attempt to roll your ball over. Upon hitting it successfully with good execution, your partner should record the results at impact in the second frame of the second game line.

*Using the Target Line:* Repeat these procedures until you find the proper target line for hitting the pocket, the 17th board. Then attempt to hit the pocket four times in a row before you run out of frames in the trial game. Your partner will judge a pocket hit. You may stop within a game as soon as you have made four pocket hits in a row within a game or when you have completed 10 frames, whichever occurs first.

**Success Goal** = 4 pocket hits in a row within a single trial game, or completion of 3 trial games ___

**Trial games**

| 1 | 2 | 3 |
|---|---|---|
| ___ | ___ | ___ |

✔ **Success Check**
• Normal setup at correct location ___
• Normal hook-ball delivery ___
• Second-arrow target ___
• Bowl as consistently as you can ___

**To Increase Difficulty**
• After 4 pocket hits in a row, bowl as many pocket hits as you can, continuing the game past 10 frames if necessary. You must miss the pocket before moving on to the next game.

**To Decrease Difficulty**
• Move on to the next game after only 2 or 3 pocket hits in a row.

## STRIKE-TARGETING SUCCESS SUMMARY

The success of a targeting system depends on how well you execute your movements. To check on your ability to use targets intelligently, ask your teacher, coach, or a trained observer to qualitatively evaluate your technique according to the flowchart found in Figure 6.11. Because this is a mental checklist, you'll need to declare your choices and intentions to your observer during your evaluation.

# STEP 7

## SPARE TARGETING: PICKING UP THE LEFTOVERS

ow important are spares? Think of it this way: if you made strikes in all of the odd-numbered frames in a game and missed a single pin spare in all of the even-numbered frames, you could not bowl 200—even though you struck half of the time! Your score would be 140! If you never strike in a game, but pick up a single-pin spare in every frame, your score would be 190.

You have been consistently rolling your straight ball or hook ball along a target line. Now, you apply that skill to the second ball of a frame to try to knock down all the pins left standing after your strike-ball. *Spare targeting* is basically identical to strike targeting, with one important exception: the desired pin impact point often changes with each spare leave.

## Why Is Spare Targeting Important?

In order to be a well-rounded bowler, you must be able to *pick up (cover,* or *convert) any* reasonable spare leave you may encounter. You must put as much thought and effort into picking up spares as you put into making strikes. Regardless of the type of competition, if you patiently and persistently convert your spares, you can avoid really low games and stay in the running until you begin to strike more frequently.

Spare leaves provide an element of variety, and you should think of them as opportunities to become more accurate and versatile. If you set your mind this way and are willing to remember some simple rules and numbers, you will become a superior spare bowler.

## How To Execute Spare Targeting

There are approximately 250 common spare leaves you can encounter, but this number becomes manageable when you realize that there are only a few angles from which all of them may be converted. Once you have properly aligned your straight or hook ball for a strike, the adjustments you must make for spare targeting are of the same proportion and direction. In other words, it matters little whether you roll a straight ball or a hook ball; the adjustments for spares are similar.

You can make some spares, called *pocket spares,* by shooting your strike target line, in which case no adjustment is necessary. Other leaves may best be converted by moving your feet to another setup location; still others may best be made by moving your target point (and, thus, your visual target) and your feet.

In this step, you will again use the second arrow as your strike target. However, when you bowl on your own in a game situation, you may have to use a totally different strike target point—for example, the first arrow, the third arrow, a board between arrows, or even one of the small dots between the foul line and the arrows. Regardless of what your target point is, you will be using some target line for your strike ball.

Before attempting any spare shots, you must first be aligned properly for your strike ball. Your points of reference for all spare attempts are your strike target and the setup location appropriate for this strike target. Although you may have to make minor adjustments to some of the setup locations prescribed in the following drills, the principles you learn will apply to all game situations. One important word: always use your normal, refined delivery for spare shots, just as for your strike shots. There is no reason to change form in an attempt to make any spare. *Use the same delivery as you do when attempting strikes; otherwise, you may corrupt your next strike shot.*

## Spare Principles

Learn the following principles thoroughly. They will make you a better spare bowler by allowing you to play spares through intelligent planning, thus increasing the probability of your spare conversion before you roll your ball. While reading these principles, look at a diagram, a picture, or an actual full rack of pins and try to identify the pins being discussed.

1. If your spare leave is to the inside, move your setup location to the outside; if the leave is outside, move your setup to the inside (see Figure 7.1).

2. Always choose a spare impact point that allows your ball to hit the pin closest to you first (see Figure 7.2).

3. Always walk toward your spare leave target; walk parallel with your spare target line (see Figure 7.3).

4. Always choose a spare impact point that allows your *ball* to contact the most pins. This practice minimizes the chance of hitting only the front pins while missing the ones farther back (called *chopping*). Unless you are attempting to *convert* a *split* (a leave in which more than one pin is missing between two

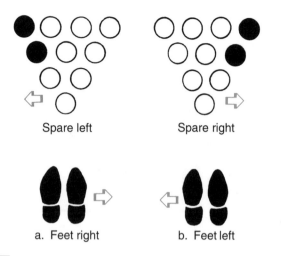

a. Feet right      b. Feet left

**Figure 7.1** Move in the proper direction for spares.

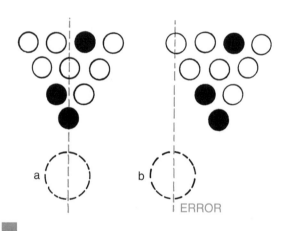

**Figure 7.2** Spare impact point: (a) correct placement; (b) incorrect placement.

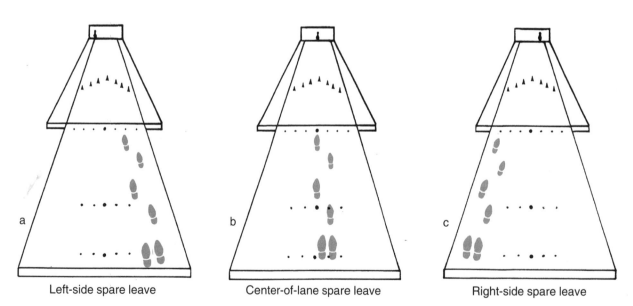

Left-side spare leave      Center-of-lane spare leave      Right-side spare leave

**Figure 7.3** Walk toward your spare leave.

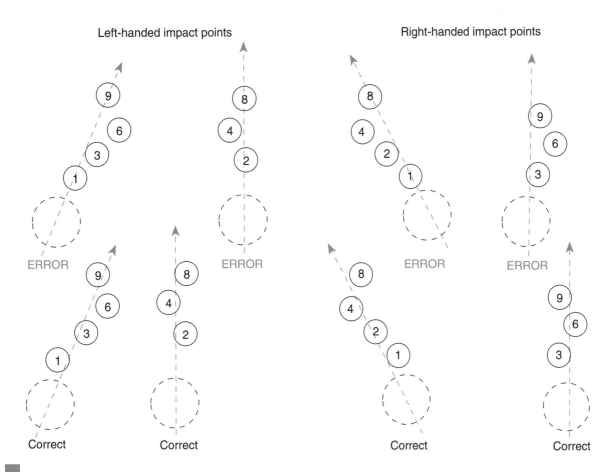

Left-handed impact points

Right-handed impact points

ERROR ERROR ERROR ERROR

Correct Correct Correct Correct

**Figure 7.4** Spare impact points: ball should contact the most pins in a spare leave; incorrect impact point shown on top; correct impact point shown on bottom.

a

or

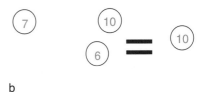

b

**Figure 7.5** Translate the spare into an easier one.

standing pins) do not depend on your ball to *carom*, or bounce, pins into other pins to make spares (see Figure 7.4).

5. Always first *translate* your spare leave into a simple one before deciding on how to shoot it. The pin leave to which it is translated may not even be part of the actual combination of pins in the leave; the translation can be a *psychologically* less difficult leave. For example, the 3-10 split can be translated as the much easier 6-pin shot because the ball will contact both the 3 pin and the 10 pin by rolling down the board upon which the 6 pin rests. Likewise, the 5-

10 split translates as a 2-pin shot, the 2-4-5-8 as an 8-pin shot, the 4-10 split as a 7-pin shot, and so on (see Figure 7.5).

6. After you have translated your spare leave, fit to it one of the seven spare target lines (detailed later in the Drills), then make appropriate adjustments of your target line and setup location from your original strike target line (see Figure 7.6).

Effective spare targeting using the target line system is nothing more than becoming skilled at carrying out the activities of the checklist illustrated in Figure 7.7.

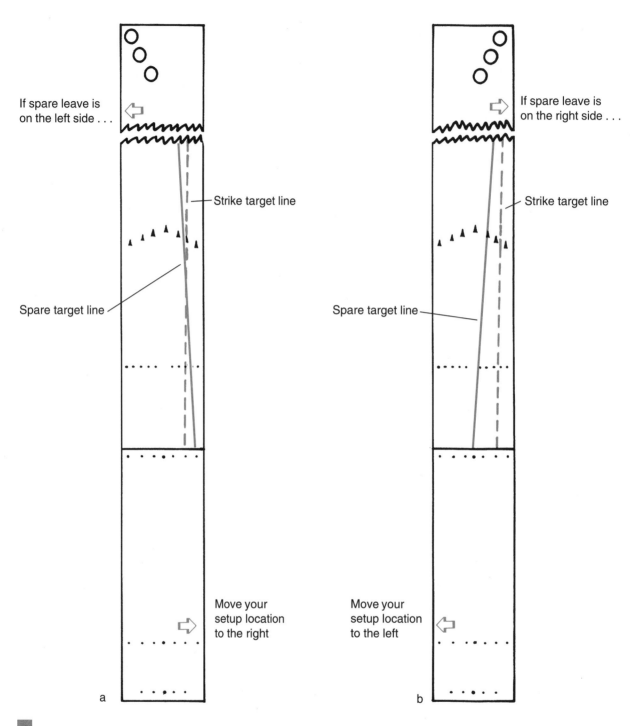

**Figure 7.6** Adjust your target line to each particular spare.

FIGURE
7.7  **KEYS TO SUCCESS**

# SPARE TARGETING SYSTEM

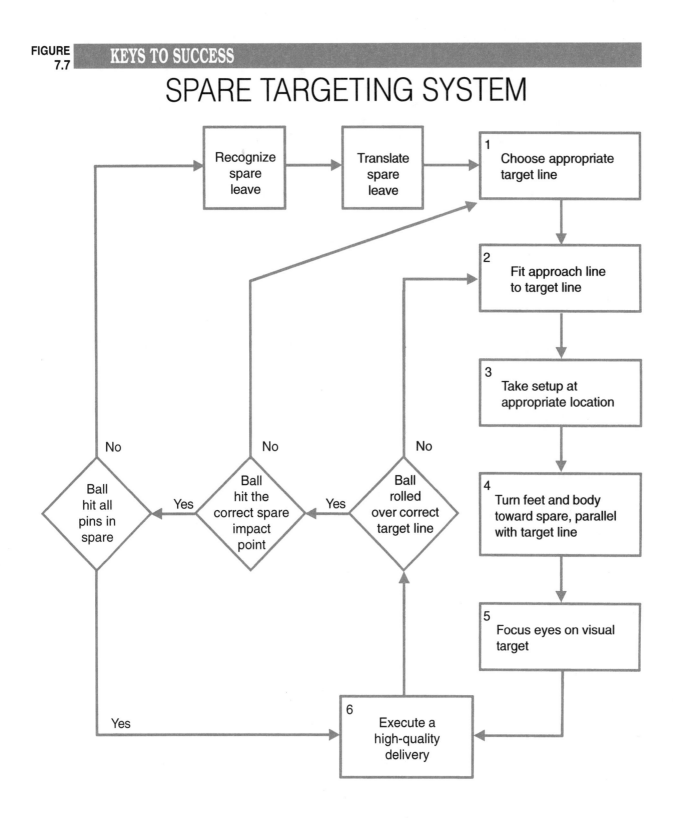

## LEAGUE AND TOURNAMENT SUCCESS STOPPERS

Common errors in spare targeting have been considered in the foregoing principles. If you strictly adhere to these principles before stepping up onto the approach to attempt a spare, you will minimize spare-targeting errors significantly. If you do not, you may attempt a spare using a poorly selected target line, thereby missing the spare before you ever roll the ball.

Any errors that occur after you have chosen the correct spare impact point and a correct target line would involve general problems in hitting any target line. For solutions to these problems, refer to the "Success Stoppers" sections of Step 6 for applicable information; simply substitute the words *"spare"* for *"strike"* and *"spare impact point"* for *"pocket"* or *"strike pocket"* in those examples. For more information on spare targeting, see Ritger and Allen (1978).

## SPARE-TARGETING

# DRILLS

In the following drills, it is assumed that the visual target for the strike ball is the second arrow from the swingside channel. For anyone using a straight ball, all of the adjustments will work effectively. For those using hook balls, however, a common strike-ball visual target may be the first arrow, the second, the third, and so on. Regardless of which strike-ball visual target is used, the "change in setup location" will work relative to the visual target, as long as the friction on the lane (the lane condition) is uniform from side to side.

*Note*: On modern lane conditions, there may be more oil dressing (less friction) in the center of the lane than on the outside edges, making spare-shooting very tricky with the hook ball. In this case, no matter which visual target you actually use for a strike, assume that you are adjusting from a second-arrow strike target. *Use a second-arrow target for shooting spares from the pocket toward the inside and a third-arrow target for spares to the outside of the pocket.* Use a straight ball or a very small hook (changing only your hand position) for all spares. This technique will pay off in a higher percentage of spares converted.

## 1. Pocket Spares

### Left-Handed Bowler

**Category:** 1-pin and 5-pin single and combination leaves
**Common examples:** 1, 5, 1-2, 1-5, 1-10, 1-8, 1-3-5, 1-3-8, 1-2-5, 1-2-4, 1-2-8, 1-2-4-7, 2-5, 5-8, 5-9
**Spare impact point:** Strike pocket

### Right-Handed Bowler

**Category:** 1-pin and 5-pin single and combination leaves
**Common examples:** 1, 5, 1-3, 1-5, 1-7, 1-9, 1-2-5, 1-2-9, 1-3-5, 1-3-6, 1-3-9, 1-3-6-10, 3-5, 5-8, 5-9
**Spare impact point:** Strike pocket

**Left-Handed Bowler**          **Right-Handed Bowler**

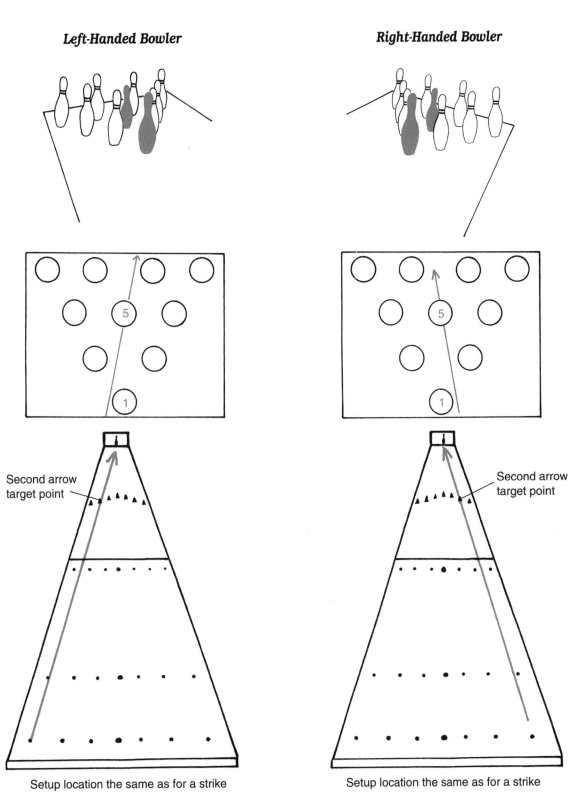

Second arrow
target point

Second arrow
target point

Setup location the same as for a strike          Setup location the same as for a strike

### All Bowlers

**Spare impact point:** The strike pocket
**Change in visual target:** None (still the second arrow)
**Change in setup location:** None

Prepare a scoresheet, using the Sample Scoresheet as a model.

### Sample Scoresheet

Deliver your ball at a full rack of pins, disregarding pin reaction. If you hit the pocket squarely, put a "+" in the small box in the upper right corner of the appropriate frame of your scoresheet; if not, enter a "–" sign. Do not, however, record any entry unless you executed your shot well and hit your spare-target line. Have a partner observe you if necessary.

Make 1-board adjustments to your setup location if necessary, and record the new setup location in the appropriate frame. In the space provided, write the board number of the setup location that allows you the most accuracy.

Repeat this procedure until you hit the pocket squarely 3 times in succession with proper execution each time, then go to the next drill. Because you will use the same scoresheet and continue from one drill to the other on the same game line, your ideal is to have all "+" entries from the first to the last frames for all of the drills.

Desired pin impact board number

Write: "+" if you hit the pocket (board #17) "–" if you did not

| NAME | 1 | 2 | 3 | 4 | 5 | 6 | 7 | 8 | 9 | 10 |
|------|---|---|---|---|---|---|---|---|---|----|
| Jane | 17 – | 17 – | 17 – | 17 + | 17 + | 17 + | | | | |
| | 18 | 19 | 20 | 21 | 21 | 21 | | | | |

Setup location

Three plus entries in a row allow you to go to next drill

### Success Goal =

a. In the following space, write your most accurate setup location (+ or –) _____ boards from the strike-target setup location

b. Hit the selected spare impact point 3 times in 3 attempts ___

### Success Check

• Translate spare ___
• Strike-ball visual target (e.g., second arrow) ___
• Strike-ball setup location ___
• Normal delivery ___

### To Increase Difficulty

• Make 4 or 5 correct consecutive hits before moving on to the next drill.

### To Decrease Difficulty

• Make only 2 successful hits before moving on to the next drill.
• Allow any quality of contact with the spare impact pin to be a successful spare attempt.

## *2. Near-Inside (Balance Side) Spares*

### *Left-Handed Bowler*

**Category:** 3-pin single and combination leaves
**Common examples:** 1, 3, 9, 1-7, 3-5, 3-6, 3-9, 1-3-6, 1-3-7, 1-3-9, 1-3-10, 3-5-6, 1-3-6-7, 1-3-6-10, 3-5-6-9, 5-6
**Spare impact point:** 3 pin

### *Right-Handed Bowler*

**Category:** 2-pin single and combination leaves
**Common examples:** 1, 2, 8, 1-10, 2-4, 2-5, 2-8, 1-2-4, 1-2-7, 1-2-8, 1-2-10, 2-4-5, 1-2-4-7, 1-2-4-10, 2-4-5-8, 4-5
**Spare impact point:** 2 pin

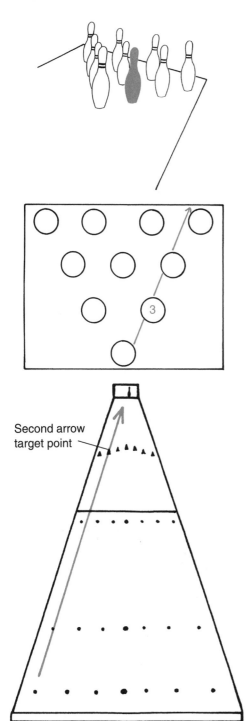

Second arrow target point

Setup location moved four boards outside

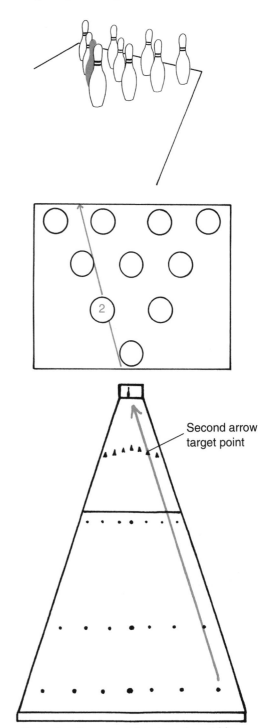

Second arrow target point

Setup location moved four boards outside

*All Bowlers*

**Change in visual target:** None (still the second arrow)
**Change in setup location:** 4 boards to the outside (–4)

Continue using the same scoresheet from the previous drill, keeping score in the same way. With the 2 pin (RH) or 3 pin (LH) as your intended impact pin, use the second arrow as your target point on the lane and move your feet to a setup location 4 boards outside your strike location. Record the spare impact point and the board number of your new setup location as before. Deliver your ball properly at the full rack, recording a "+" for a square hit on the impact pin and a "–" for any other type of hit.

Make 1-board adjustments to your setup location if necessary, and record the new setup location in the appropriate frame. In the space provided, write the board number of the setup location that allows you the most accuracy.

Repeat this drill until you hit the pin squarely 3 times in succession, then proceed to the next drill. Are you on your way to all "+" entries?

### Success Goal =

a. In the following space, write your most accurate setup location (+ or –) _____ boards from the strike-target setup location

b. Hit the selected spare impact point 3 times in 3 attempts ___

### ✔ Success Check

• Translate spare ___
• Second arrow visual target ___
• Take setup 4 boards to outside of strike location ___
• Normal delivery ___

### To Increase Difficulty

• Make 4 or 5 correct consecutive hits before moving on to the next drill.

### To Decrease Difficulty

• Make only 2 successful hits before moving on to the next drill.
• Allow any quality of contact with the spare impact pin to be a successful spare attempt.

## 3. Medium-Inside (Balance Side) Spares

| *Left-Handed Bowler* | *Right-Handed Bowler* |
|---|---|
| **Category:** 6-pin single and combination leaves | **Category:** 4-pin single and combination leaves |
| **Common examples:** 6, 6-9, 6-10, 3-7, 3-10, 3-5-6 | **Common examples:** 4, 4-7, 4-8, 2-7, 2-10, 2-4-5 |
| **Spare impact point:** 6 pin | **Spare impact point:** 4 pin |

### Left-Handed Bowler

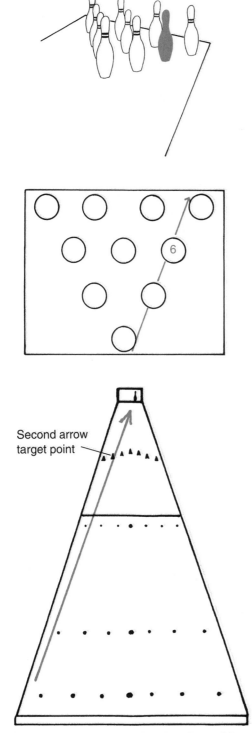

### Right-Handed Bowler

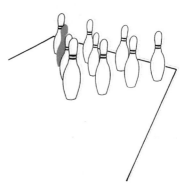

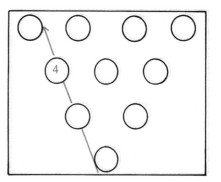

Second arrow
target point

Second arrow
target point

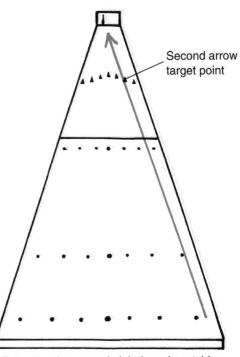

Setup location moved eight boards outside

Setup location moved eight boards outside

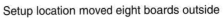

### All Bowlers

**Change in visual target:** None (still the second arrow)
**Change in setup location:** 8 boards to the outside (–8)

With the 4 pin (RH) or 6 pin (LH) as your intended impact pin, use the second arrow as your target point on the lane and move your feet to a setup location 8 boards outside your strike location. Record the spare impact point and the board number of your new setup location. Deliver your ball at a full rack, making entries as before. Make and record adjustments in your setup location as in the previous drills.

Repeat this drill until you hit the pin squarely 3 times in succession, then proceed to the next drill. How long is your string of "+" entries?

### Success Goal =

a. In the following space, write your most accurate setup location (+ or –) _____ boards from the strike-target setup location

b. Hit the selected spare impact point 3 times in 3 attempts ___

### Success Check

• Translate spare ___
• Second-arrow visual target ___
• Take setup 8 boards to outside of strike location ___
• Normal delivery ___

### To Increase Difficulty

• Make 4 or 5 correct consecutive hits before moving on to the next drill.

### To Decrease Difficulty

• Make only 2 successful hits before moving on to the next drill.
• Allow any quality of contact with the spare impact pin to be a successful spare attempt.

## 4. Far-Inside (Balance Side) Corner Pin Spares

### Left-Handed Bowler

**Category:** 10-pin single
**Common examples:** 10, 6-7, 6-8, 6-7-10, 6-8-10
**Spare impact point:** 10 pin

### Right-Handed Bowler

**Category:** 7-pin single
**Common examples:** 7, 4-9, 4-10, 4-7-9, 4-7-10
**Spare impact point:** 7 pin

### *Left-Handed Bowler*

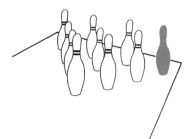

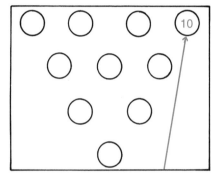

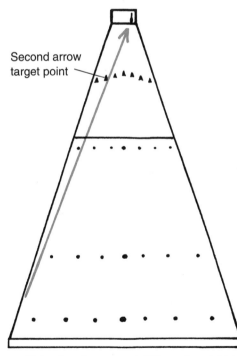

Second arrow
target point

Setup location moved 12 boards outside

### *Right-Handed Bowler*

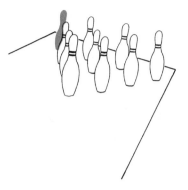

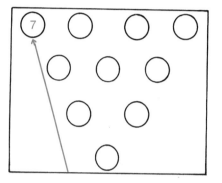

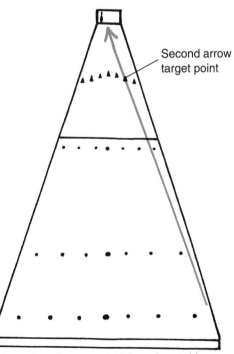

Second arrow
target point

Setup location moved 12 boards outside

*All Bowlers*

**Change in visual target:** None (still the second arrow)
**Change in setup location:** 12 boards to the outside (–12)

With the 7 pin (RH) or 10 pin (LH) as your intended impact pin, use the second arrow as your target point on the lane and move your feet to a setup location 12 boards outside your strike location. Record the spare impact point and the board number of your new setup location. Deliver your ball at a full rack, making entries as before. Make and record adjustments in your setup location as before.

Repeat this drill until you hit the pin squarely 3 times in succession, then proceed to the next drill. Are you stringing together "+" entries?

### Success Goal =

a. In the following space, write your most accurate setup location (+ or –) _____ boards from the strike-target setup location

b. Hit the selected spare impact point 3 times in 3 attempts ___

### Success Check

- Translate spare ___
- Second-arrow visual target ___
- Take setup 12 boards to outside of strike location ___
- Normal delivery ___

### To Increase Difficulty

- Make 4 or 5 correct consecutive hits before moving on to the next drill.

### To Decrease Difficulty

- Make only 2 successful hits before moving on to the next drill.
- Allow any quality of contact with the spare impact pin to be a successful spare attempt.

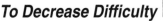

## 5. Near-Outside (Swingside) Spares

*Left-Handed Bowler*

**Category:** 2-pin single and combination leaves
**Common examples:** 2, 8, 2-4, 2-5, 2-8, 4-5, 5-10, 2-4-5, 2-4-7, 2-4-8, 2-5-8, 2-4-5-8
**Spare impact point:** 2 pin

*Right-Handed Bowler*

**Category:** 3-pin single and combination leaves
**Common examples:** 3, 9, 3-5, 3-6, 3-9, 5-6, 5-7, 3-5-6, 3-5-9, 3-6-9, 3-6-10, 3-5-6-9
**Spare impact point:** 3 pin

### *Left-Handed Bowler*

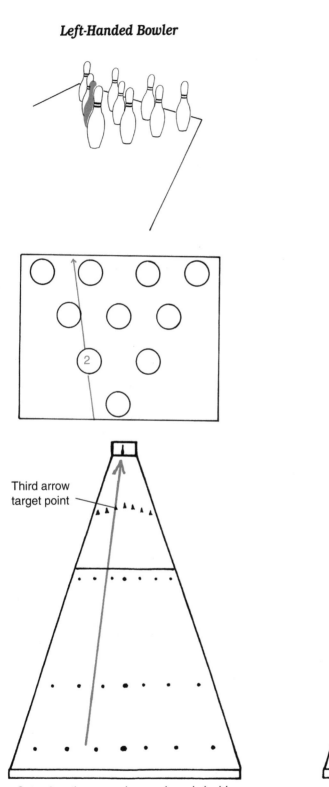

Third arrow
target point

Setup location moved seven boards inside

### *Right-Handed Bowler*

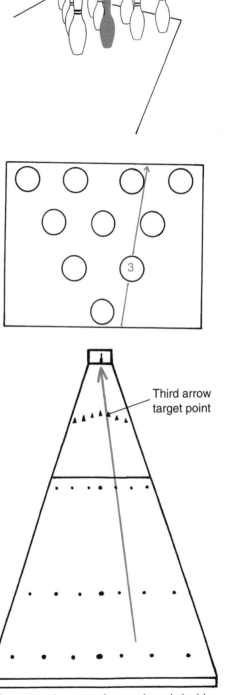

Third arrow
target point

Setup location moved seven boards inside

### All Bowlers

**Change in visual target:** To third arrow (+5)
**Change in setup location:** 7 boards to the inside (+7)

With the 3 pin (RH) or 2 pin (LH) as your intended impact pin, use the third arrow as your target point on the lane and move your feet to a setup location 7 boards inside your strike location. Record the spare impact point and the board number of your new setup location. Deliver your ball at a full rack, making entries as before. Make and record adjustments in your setup location as before.

Repeat this drill until you hit the pin squarely 3 times in succession, then proceed to the next drill. How are the "+" entries coming along?

### Success Goal =

a. In the following space, write your most accurate setup location (+ or –) _____ boards from the strike-target setup location

b. Hit the selected spare impact point 3 times in 3 attempts ___

### Success Check

- Translate spare ___
- Third arrow visual target ___
- Take setup 7 boards to inside of strike location ___
- Normal delivery ___

### To Increase Difficulty

- Make 4 or 5 correct consecutive hits before moving on to the next drill.

### To Decrease Difficulty

- Make only 2 successful hits before moving on to the next drill.
- Allow any quality of contact with the spare impact pin to be a successful spare attempt.

## 6. Medium-Outside (Swingside) Spares

### Left-Handed Bowler

**Category:** 4-pin single and combination leaves
**Common examples:** 4, 2-7, 2-10, 4-7, 4-8, 2-7-10
**Spare impact point:** 4 pin

### Right-Handed Bowler

**Category:** 6-pin single and combination leaves
**Common examples:** 6, 3-7, 3-10, 6-9, 6-10, 3-7-10
**Spare impact point:** 6 pin

### *Left-Handed Bowler*                    ### *Right-Handed Bowler*

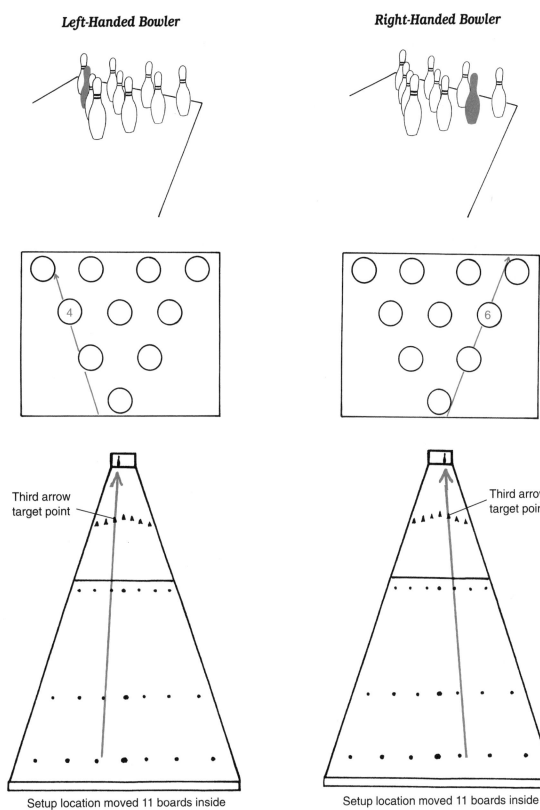

Third arrow
target point

Third arrow
target point

Setup location moved 11 boards inside                    Setup location moved 11 boards inside

### All Bowlers

**Change in visual target:** To third arrow (+5)
**Change in setup location:** 11 boards to the inside (+11)

With the 6 pin (RH) or 4 pin (LH) as your intended impact pin, use the third arrow as your target point on the lane and move your feet to a setup location 11 boards inside your strike location. Record the spare impact point and the board number of your new setup location. Deliver your ball at a full rack, making entries as before. Make and record adjustments to your setup location as before.

### Success Goal =

a. In the following space, write your most accurate setup location (+ or –) _____ boards from the strike-target setup location

b. Hit the selected spare impact point 3 times in 3 attempts ___

### Success Check

- Translate spare ___
- Third-arrow visual target ___
- Take setup 11 boards to inside of strike location ___
- Normal delivery ___

### To Increase Difficulty

- Make 4 or 5 correct consecutive hits before moving on to the next drill.

### To Decrease Difficulty

- Make only 2 successful hits before moving on to the next drill.
- Allow any quality of contact with the spare impact pin to be a successful spare attempt.

## 7. Far-Outside (Swingside) Corner Pin Spares

### Left-Handed Bowler

**Category:** 7-pin single
**Common examples:** 7, 4-6, 4-10, 4-7-10, 4-8-10
**Spare impact point:** 7 pin

### Right-Handed Bowler

**Category:** 10-pin single
**Common examples:** 10, 4-6, 6-7, 6-7-10, 6-9-10
**Spare impact point:** 10 pin

<p>

## Left-Handed Bowler

## Right-Handed Bowler

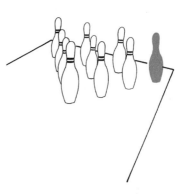

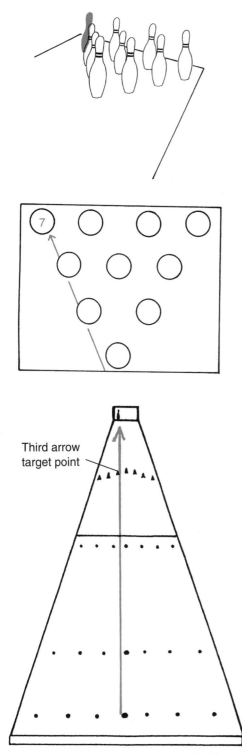

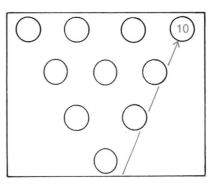

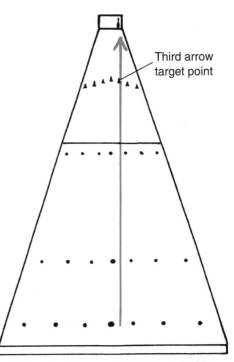

Third arrow target point

Third arrow target point

Setup location moved 13 boards inside

Setup location moved 13 boards inside

### All Bowlers
**Change in visual target:** To third arrow (+5)
**Change in setup location:** 13 boards to the inside (+13)

With the 10 pin (RH) or 7 pin (LH) as your intended impact pin, use the third arrow as your target point on the lane and move your feet to a setup location 13 boards inside your strike location. Record the spare impact point and board number of your new setup location. Roll at a full rack, as in the previous drills. Make and record adjustments in your setup location as before.

## Success Goal =

a. In the following space, write your most accurate setup location (+ or –) _____ boards from the strike-target setup location

b. Hit the selected spare impact point 3 times in 3 attempts ___

## Success Check

• Translate spare ___
• Third-arrow visual target ___
• Take setup 13 boards to inside of strike location ___
• Normal delivery ___

## To Increase Difficulty
• Make 4 or 5 correct consecutive hits before moving on to the next drill.

## To Decrease Difficulty
• Make only 2 successful hits before moving on to the next drill.
• Allow any quality of contact with the spare impact pin to be a successful spare attempt.

**Stop!** Complete the Corrected Setup Location Chart before you move on to the next drill. Transfer into the appropriate boxes the most appropriate setup locations you identified in the Success Goal section of Drills 1 through 7. Use the new, reliable setup locations on the Corrected Setup Location Chart when shooting spares along different target lines in the following "fun" drills.

**Corrected Setup Location Chart**

| Spare category | Most accurate setup location* |
|---|---|
| Pocket spares | No Change |
| Near inside | |
| Medium inside | |
| Far-inside corner pin | |
| Near outside | |
| Medium outside | |
| Far-outside corner pin | |

*Expressed by number of boards inside (+) or outside (–) the strike setup location.

## 8. Spare Cleanup

Bowl three games with a partner. In the first frame of the first game, your partner will roll the first ball, practicing good strike-targeting technique. You will attempt to pick up any remaining pins. In the second frame, you roll the first ball and let your partner convert the spare. Continue alternating throughout the three games.

After each game, divide the number of successful spare conversions by the number of times you attempted to make a spare. Multiply this number by 100 to obtain a percentage score that will help you track your success.

**Success Goal** = 80% spare conversion in any one game; use the following chart to record your success

|  | Game number | | |
|---|---|---|---|
|  | 1 | 2 | 3 |
| Success Rate = (%) conversion | ____ | ____ | ____ |

### To Increase Difficulty

- Try a cutthroat variation—on each first ball, attempt to leave the most difficult spares for your partner to convert. Try your best to beat your partner. Balls rolled into the channel count as a strike for your partner!

### Success Check

- Bowl 3 games ___
- Normal delivery ___
- Use correct strike-targeting technique ___
- Use correct spare-targeting technique ___
- Try to be accurate ___

## 9. Corner-Pin Sharpshooter

This game involves a high degree of spare-shooting accuracy and some competition. You can play this game in competition against one opponent, or you can team up with a partner and bowl against two opponents, adding your two games to get one doubles-team score. Many variations are possible; you may make up some of your own. Keep your score on a regular scoresheet, but write only points (as follows)—not strikes, spares, or regular pinfall—in the frames.

*Point values:*

- 7 pin and 10 pin = 10 points each pin
- 4-7-8 and 6-9-10 = 5 points for all three pins
- Knocking down any other pin = 0 points for the attempt (includes striking on the first or second ball)
- Ball rolled into channel = minus (–) 20 points

The objective of each frame is to roll a first ball and a second ball, knocking down only the 7 pin and the 10 pin with two shots; this method will give you a score of 20 in the frame.

Less accuracy may result in your knocking down the 4-7-8 and 6-9-10 combinations, yielding a total score of 10 in the frame. Knocking down the 10 pin and then the 4-6-8 would give you 15 points in the frame; however, knocking down the 10 pin and then knocking down the 6-9 would reduce the score from 10 to 5 (5 being the value of knocking down the 6-9-10 together).

Rolling a ball into the channel on the first attempt (–20) and then hitting only the 7 pin on the second ball (+10) would give a –10 (– 20 + 10) for the frame. Only 2 balls are allowed in the tenth frame (see the Scored Frames Example).

**Scored Frames Example**

| | | | | | | | | | | | | | | | | | | | | |
|---|---|---|---|---|---|---|---|---|---|---|---|---|---|---|---|---|---|---|---|---|
| **Bill/Carla** | 10 | 10 | 5 | 0 | 10 | 10 | 10 | –20 | 5 | 5 | –20 | 5 | 10 | 10 | 10 | 5 | 10 | 5 | 5 | 5 |
| | 20 | | 25 | | 45 | | 35 | | 45 | | 30 | | 50 | | 65 | | 80 | | 90 | |
| **Holly/Kim** | –20 | 10 | 10 | 5 | 10 | 5 | 10 | 10 | 0 | 5 | 5 | 5 | 5 | 0 | 10 | 10 | –20 | 10 | 10 | 5 |
| | –10 | | 5 | | 20 | | 40 | | 45 | | 55 | | 60 | | 80 | | 70 | | 85 | |

**Success Goal** = Outscore your opponent with as high a score as you can bowl (200 points maximum); use the following chart to record your success

|  | **Game number** | | | |
|---|---|---|---|---|
| | 1 | 2 | 3 | 4 |
| Yourself (points) = | ___ | ___ | ___ | ___ |
| Opponent (points) = | ___ | ___ | ___ | ___ |

**✔ Success Check**
- Bowl 4 games ___
- Normal delivery ___
- Use correct spare-targeting technique ___
- Roll at corner pins only ___
- Try to be accurate ___

**To Increase Difficulty**
- Right-handers can either knock down the 7 pin first or not be given a chance to roll at the 10 pin. Left-handers can either knock down the 10 pin first or not be given a chance to roll at the 7 pin. Subtract 5 points any time a ball hits the 4-7-8 or 6-9-10.

**To Decrease Difficulty**
- Bowl only 2 or 3 games.

## 10. Bowling Bingo

This version of the familiar Bingo game features first-ball pinfall as the number to be entered into Bowling Bingo squares on a prepared scoresheet.

*Scoresheet Preparation:* A heavy line is drawn on the division between the fifth and sixth frames, and another heavy line is drawn between the fifth and sixth games (see Appendix Scoresheet). The result is four "Bowling Bingo cards" consisting of 25 frames each. Mark the frames as shown in the Sample Scoresheet for Bingo.

**Sample Scoresheet for Bingo**

| 2-4 | 5-8 | 9-12 | 13-16 | 17-20 |
|------|------|------|------|------|
| 2 | Free | 10 | 14 | 20 |
| 4 | 7 | 12 | 16 | Free |
| 2 | 6 | Free | 15 | 17 |
| Free | 5 | 9 | 13 | 18 |
| 3 | 8 | 11 | Free | 19 |

*Rules:* The two teams on each pair of lanes join forces and compete against other paired teams. Teams on lanes 1 and 2 are called "Pair l," those on lanes 3 and 4 are called "Pair 2," and so on. Each team pair uses one Bowling Bingo card for each game.

All bowlers on the teams participate in bowling only first balls to achieve pin count. The remaining pins are then swept off the pin deck. Bowlers should not race; bowling proceeds at the usual pace, and normal lane courtesy should be observed.

The number in the Bowling Bingo squares range from 2 to 20. The leadoff bowlers from both teams roll first balls, and the scorekeeper adds the two pinfall counts together. If this pinfall count total matches one of the numbers on the Bowling Bingo card, the scorekeeper crosses out the number with a heavy **X**. Only one occurrence of a number on a card may be crossed out per two-bowler attempt. Sweep any remaining pins off the deck.

The next-up bowlers from both teams follow, rolling only first balls. The total of the two bowlers' first balls is compared with the Bowling Bingo card; the scorekeeper crosses out the next number. This rotation continues until a team pair has **X** entries—either across, down, diagonally, or in one of the patterns shown in the examples below—on its Bowling Bingo card. When the team pair has "made Bingo," some (or all) of the members should shout, "Bingo!" At this point the game ends.

**Example Bingo Patterns**

**Success Goal** = Bowl 2 games of Bowling Bingo ___

**Success Check**
- Normal delivery ___
- Use correct spare-targeting technique ___
- Roll only at number of pins needed ___
- Score points for accuracy ___

**To Increase Difficulty**
- Additional patterns may be used to provide variety (see Example Bingo Patterns).

**To Decrease Difficulty**
- Allow + or – one pin to be a successful pinfall. For example, if the shot requires a 3-pin count, allow a 2- or 4-pin count to be a 3-pin count.

## 11. Cutthroat Crossover

This is an amusing game of tactics to undermine the opponents. It also involves a variety of spare-shooting skills.

*Rules*: Two teams compete against each other on a pair of lanes. Unlike regulation team competition, all bowlers on a team participate together in bowling only one, single gameline. The gameline on the odd lane is the odd team's score, and the gameline on the even lane is the even team's score.

The amusing feature of this game is that the leadoff bowler of one team bowls the first ball of the other team's leadoff bowler's frame! Then the next bowler from each team switches to the correct lane to try to pick up the spare. The second member of the opposing team bowls the first ball of the second frame, and so on. A strike counts for the opposing team, so be careful!

*Objective*: To outscore the opposing team in a regulation single game. One important rule, though: A first ball rolled into the channel counts as a strike for the team in whose frame it was rolled, so a team should not try to low-ball the opposing team into a low score. It is advantageous to keep the ball on the lane. A sharpshooter might try for a corner pin, leaving nine pins for the opposition's spare. A daring first-ball bowler might even try to create a split, at the risk of high pinfall or even an inadvertent strike.

**Success Goal** = 2 games of Cutthroat Crossover, winning both ___

|  | Game | | |
|---|---|---|---|
|  | 1 | 2 | Total |
| Your Team's Score (points) = | ___ | ___ | ___ |
| Opposing Team's Score (points) = | ___ | ___ | ___ |

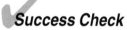

**Success Check**
- Bowl in teams ___
- Use correct spare-targeting technique ___
- Normal delivery ___
- Bowl your opponent's first ball ___

**To Increase Difficulty**
- Allow the opposing team to choose the bowler from the opposite team who will shoot the spare. Ideally, the worst spare bowler will be chosen and will improve with the additional practice.

**To Decrease Difficulty**
- If teams are unbalanced, add handicap to the lower-average team's score.

### 12. Tic-Tac-Bowl

This is another "fun" accuracy game that depends on the strike- and spare-targeting abilities of all participants. The objective is the same as the traditional Tic-Tac-Toe game—to get 3 X or O entries in a row, horizontally, vertically, or diagonally on the game board. The right to place an X or an O on the board is earned by making correct first- and second-ball attempts, that is, making marks. It is very fast-paced, since a game can be won in three shots.

*Rules*: Competition is on a pair of lanes, with either individuals or teams (hereafter called players) competing against each other. Players assigned the X entries are called X players, or simply X; players assigned the O entries are called O players, or simply O. Players may either remain on one lane of the pair or alternate lanes.

Toss a coin to decide who starts first. Then, X and O alternate two balls, each attempting to get a strike. The first player to either get a strike or convert the spare gets to place a mark on the Tic-Tac-Bowl board.

**Success Goal** = Complete 3 or more games of Tic-Tac-Bowl, attempting to get 3 X or 3 O entries horizontally, vertically, or diagonally on the game board ___

**Success Check**
- Normal delivery ___
- Use correct strike-targeting technique ___
- Use correct spare-targeting technique ___
- Try to strike and spare ___
- Score an X or O for a mark ___

**To Increase Difficulty**
- Count only 8-count spares and above. Bowl the frame over if both players do not count at least 8 on the first ball.

**To Decrease Difficulty**
- Accept only the better pin count of a frame to mark the X or O. Both opponents will bowl each frame, comparing pinfall on the first ball or total pinfall for two balls. Naturally, a strike beats a spare, even though both represent 10 pins.

## SPARE-TARGETING SUCCESS SUMMARY

Your success in using a targeting system to shoot spares depends on (1) whether you select the correct target line for the spare, and (2) how well you execute your movements. To check on your ability to shoot spares intelligently, ask your teacher, coach, or a trained observer to evaluate your technique qualitatively according to the spare principles and specific target lines found in the drills of this step.

# STEP 8

# PHYSICAL ADAPTATIONS: OVERCOMING ENVIRONMENTAL FACTORS

Have you ever seen a group of really good bowlers bowling a tournament in a hot, humid bowling center on a very difficult lane condition? You may have noticed that some struggled and gave up while others did not, even though no one seemed to be scoring very well. The ones who perform well under such conditions know what to do and keep trying until they come out on top.

So far, you have been working very hard on the physical components of your performance. Although you may not yet be a skilled bowler, you are capable of learning some refined skills that will allow you to make physical adaptations to some challenging environmental factors, while maintaining a consistent, well-executed delivery.

## Why Are Physical Adaptations Important?

Most environmental factors in bowling are beyond your control. Lane condition changes, temperature fluctuations inside the bowling center, and the friction on the approaches differ from one establishment to the next. However, the way you respond to these factors *is* under your control. If you do not respond quickly and correctly to environmental factors, you will have low scores, become frustrated, lose confidence, and carry a poor attitude into your next performance. Many high-average bowlers have unnecessarily stopped bowling because they could not adjust physically to new, unfamiliar lane conditions that could have become manageable through a sensible plan of restructuring their performance techniques to fit the new conditions.

## How To Execute Physical Adaptations

Certain physical factors in your bowling environment can exert a negative influence on your execution, altering your movement plan to a less effective one. You must recognize these factors and use correct adaptive tactics, or these alterations can become a persistent part of your movement plan, making you a less skilled bowler with bad habits. You must stay on top of the situation by (a) being aware of changes in the physical environment when they occur, (b) knowing how these changes affect your performance, and (c) using intelligent physical-adaptive tactics to offset negative effects.

You should never modify an essential part of your delivery to adapt to a temporary condition. In order not to alter your movement plan, you must know which characteristics of your delivery you may change without interfering with reliable, technically sound movements. Safe, *technique-supportive* adaptations allow you to maintain proper execution while you cope with the environmental conditions. However, if you employ unsafe, *technique-interfering* adaptations, you will induce your body to make new, potentially unsound movements. Three examples of each follow:

### Safe

1. Alteration of target line by moving feet and target point.
2. Alteration of finger position to make ball skid farther or roll sooner.
3. Alteration of ball speed by changing length of swing while retaining a good pushaway.

### Unsafe

1. Changing the direction of pushaway relative to approach line so that the swing is no longer parallel with the approach line.
2. Curling the thumb to lessen the lift at the release.
3. Muscling the swing to increase the lift at the release.

# Common Environmental Problems

Assuming that your physical and mental games are in good working order, errors in bowling can be caused by your inability to cope effectively with the physical bowling environment in some way. When the environment presents problems, you can still make a "respectable showing" by being able to diagnose the following problems correctly and employing a "safe" solution. Do not expect to be an "expert" from what you will learn in this section; new situations always arise, and you must experience them for yourself, learn from them, and deal with them better the next time.

For now, learn to analyze and correct the following common problems, and you will be on your way to developing the skills you need to stay "on top" of most situations. For each problem, there is listed a cause, and both a safe (technique-supportive adaptation) and an unsafe (technique-interfering adaptation) solution.

### Problem 1

Your thumb hangs in the thumbhole at the release, causing you to muscle the forward swing and loft the ball.

**Cause** Your hand swells due to high heat and humidity.

**Safe** Keep your thumbhole dry; if you have time, consult a pro shop operator for assistance.

**Unsafe** Do not sand or enlarge your thumbhole or finger holes unless it is absolutely necessary; the ball may not then fit properly.

### Problem 2

You are dropping the ball, and the holes feel loose.

**Cause** Your hand shrinks due to low temperature.

**Safe** Use rosin powder on the gripping surfaces of your fingers and thumb—never on the base of the thumb. Insert vinyl tape in the backs of the holes to make them smaller. Take some of the tape out as your fingers and thumb swell.

**Unsafe** Never dust rosin powder into the holes; this practice may make your thumb or fingers hang in your ball, and can cause blisters.

### Problem 3

Your sliding shoe "sticks," shortening your slide.

**Cause** The approaches become tacky due to high heat and humidity.

**Safe** Use soapstone on your sliding sole. Slow your footwork down to minimize stress on your sliding leg hip.

**Unsafe** Never apply powder to the approaches; always ask the counter control person for assistance with house factor troubles.

### Problem 4

You slip during your approach, making you feel unsteady. You waggle to the foul line and slide too far.

**Cause** The approaches become slick due to excessive dust, low humidity, or someone having used powder on them.

**Safe** Wipe your shoes often with a towel. Call for a lane maintenance person to clean the approaches.

**Unsafe** Never apply any substance to the approaches.

### Problem 5

Your ball hooks excessively.

**Cause** The lanes have developed a high-friction condition.

**Safe** See Figure 8.1. This information pertains only to the hook-ball delivery. Straight-ball dynamics are minimally affected, so the following adaptations are not relevant to a straight ball. You may use one or any combination of the following, but it is best to progress sequentially through the list.

a. Alter your target line by
- moving your feet to a more inside setup location while retaining the same target point,
- moving your target point farther outside while retaining your original setup location, or
- moving your target point outside and your setup location inside.

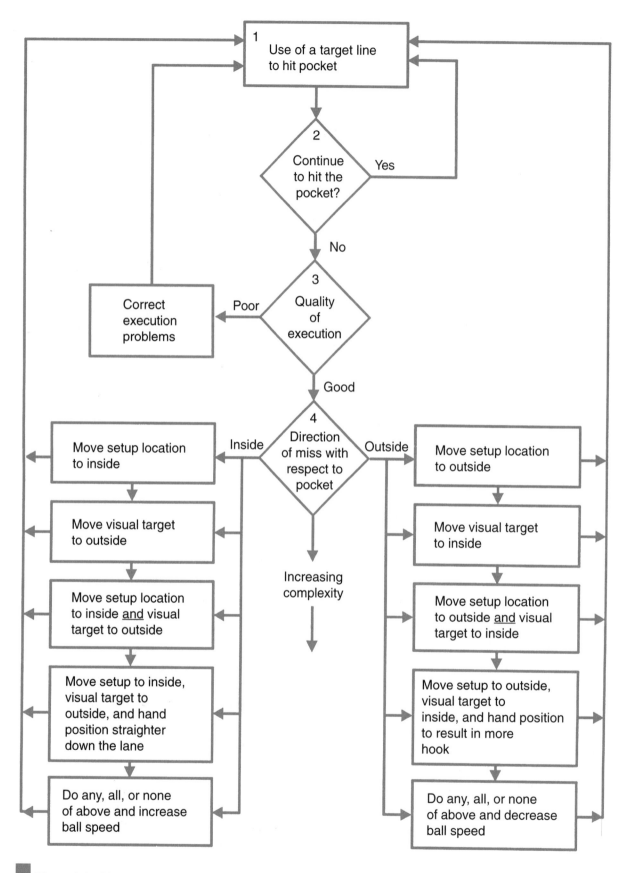

**Figure 8.1** Physical adaptation flowchart: When and how to adjust your target line for a hook ball delivery.

b. Change the dynamic, hooking characteristics of the ball by

- modifying your finger position—only between 10 o'clock and 2 o'clock (both right- and left-handed bowlers)—so that your lifting fingers are pointed more toward the pins; or
- increasing your ball speed, but only by raising the level of your extended pushaway position to increase the length of your swing. Keep your forearm up in your stance and push the ball up and straight out to a level between your chest and your shoulder. You must slow down your footwork to match the longer swing.

**Unsafe** Never muscle your downswing or forward swing to increase ball speed; muscling will destroy your pendulum swing. A common problem resulting from bowling on lanes that hook too much is fast feet combined with a tense, muscled swing. This problem allows the feet to outrun the swing; the ball then becomes even later relative to the feet, resulting in even more lift, compounding the whole problem of excessive hook!

## Problem 6

Your ball does not hook enough; it seems to skid.

**Cause** The lanes have developed a low-friction condition.

**Safe** Again, see Figure 8.1. This information pertains only to the hook-ball delivery. Straight-ball dynamics are minimally affected, so the following adaptations are not relevant to a straight ball. You may use one or any combination of the following, but it is best to progress sequentially through the list.

a. Alter your target line by

- moving your feet to a more outside set-up location while retaining the same target point,
- moving your target point inside while retaining your original setup location, or
- moving your target point inside and your setup location outside.

b. Change the dynamic, hooking characteristics of your ball by

- modifying your finger position—only between 10 o'clock and 2 o'clock (both right- and left-

handed bowlers)—so that your lifting fingers are pointed more toward your body; or

- decrease your ball speed, but only by lowering the level of your extended pushaway position to decrease the length of your swing. Keep your forearm above or parallel with the approach in your stance, and push the ball straight out from the level of your elbow; you must take slightly faster steps to match the shorter swing.

**Unsafe** Never slow your downswing or forward swing to decrease your ball speed, and never eliminate your pushaway. A common problem resulting from bowling on lanes that do not hook sufficiently is the loss of a pushaway, which must be the first ingredient in establishing a pendulum swing. Insufficient pushaway leads to hoisting the ball behind the back, accompanied by excessive bending at the waist and a weak lift with a loss of roll, a necessary pin-carrying factor. The pendulum swing, regardless of its length, is the best way to promote consistent lift.

## Problem 7

You miss the strike pocket, spare leaves, and your target—consistently to the inside.

**Immediate causes:**

- Holding your ball too close to your centerline in your setup.
- Rounding off your pushaway. The ball seems too heavy.
- Bending too much at your waist while the ball is falling into the downswing, making your ball late with respect to your footwork.
- Allowing your shoulders to swing by not keeping your balance arm extended out, down, and back.
- Allowing your swing shoulder to pull back from your swing in the forward swing. This motion is termed *opening up*, and often results in your pulling the ball to the inside and in a stifled follow-through.
- Allowing your legs to be too straight during your last step and slide.

**Cause** You are tired.

**Safe** Be especially attentive to proper technique; you must literally scramble back to basics on every shot. One obvious option is to use a lighter-weight ball.

**Unsafe** Never deviate from proper technique to cope with being tired; always move your target line if your ball is hooking too soon, but be sure that you are executing properly before you make any adjustments in your target line.

## Problem 8

You are literally running to the foul line, making your ball very late relative to the pace of your steps. You may be dropping the ball at the line, hanging on to the thumbhole too long, and missing your target to either side.

**Cause** You are excited, hyped—a concentration problem that could be resolved with long-term mental training. However, due to your lack of time in the midst of bowling a game, this problem must be coped with through short-term environmental adaptations.

**Safe** Slow your footwork down to the cadence you have learned. Keep your back straight, with your pushaway and first step well coordinated.

**Unsafe** Do not slow your footwork down without first making sure that you are using a pendulum swing. Otherwise, you will be attempting to fit slow footwork to a fast swing!

---

**PHYSICAL ADAPTATION**

# DRILLS

## 1. Adaptive Situation Awareness

Learn to make logical choices in adjusting to changing lane conditions. Study the flowchart in Figure 8.1, noting all relationships among the various boxes and decision point diamonds. When you feel that you are ready, answer the following questions, referring to the flowchart yourself. Give yourself 1 point for each correct answer.

### Adjustment Quiz

a. If you are hitting the pocket consistently with your present target line, what should you do?

b. You are contentedly hitting your successful target line; what is the first element you should analyze?

c. If your ball is beginning to miss the pocket, and you are not executing properly, what should you do next?

d. If your ball is beginning to miss the pocket, but you are sure that you are executing properly, what is the first thing you should do?

e. If you have changed your setup location and your ball is still missing the pocket, what should you do next?

f. If you have moved your setup location a reasonable amount (e.g., 5 boards) and your ball is still missing the pocket, and you are sure that you are executing properly, what should you try next?

g. Arrange the following adaptations in order from simple to complex:

1. Move both setup location and target point.

2. Move setup location, target point, and your finger position.

3. Move only your setup location.

4. Move only your target point.

5. Change your ball speed.

**Success Goal** = 7 out of 7 points ___

**Success Check**
- Study Figure 8.1 ___
- Discuss the logic with your partner ___
- Answer quiz questions ___
- Check your answers ___

**To Increase Difficulty**
- Answer the questions without looking at the flow-chart.

**To Decrease Difficulty**
- Discuss the underlying logic with a partner who has looked at the answers. Allow the partner to question you.

## Adjustment Quiz Answer Key

a. Continue using the same target line.

b. Your execution.

c. Correct the execution problems and try the same target line again.

d. Move only your setup location in the same direction as the error; leave your target point unchanged, and try the new target line by rolling a ball (simplest adaptation).

e. Check to see whether you are executing properly. Trace the flow down through the chart from the top again; the chart will direct you to correct any execution problems and to try the same target line again.

f. Move your target point in the opposite direction and try the new target line by rolling a ball (a more complex adaptation). Your next option could be to move both the target point and the setup location (a still more complex adaptation).

g. 3, 4, 1, 2, 5

## 2. Target-Line Shift

Learn how to shift your target systematically. You will roll trial games consisting of 10 first balls. Take a warm-up before beginning and ensure proper execution. Use different visual strike targets and setup locations. Your partner will act as observer to tell you after each attempt whether you actually rolled your ball over your intended target line.

You may find it necessary to attempt a frame's first ball more than once, to make sure that you hit the designated target line and you executed properly before making an entry in the scoresheet frame. Give yourself an automatic spare and sweep all remaining pins off of the deck.

Prepare a scoresheet, using the Sample Scoresheet as a model.

**Sample Scoresheet**

| Target line | | | | | | | | | | |
|---|---|---|---|---|---|---|---|---|---|---|
| Impact point | | | | | | | | | | |

a. *Finding the Line Using One Target Point*: Write a "10" on one side of the diagonal in frame 1 and a "10" on the other side of the diagonal in the same frame.

Take your setup on the appropriate board for your 10-to-10 target line and roll first balls.

Change your setup location if necessary, using the 3-0-1-2 system, until you hit the pocket.

Continue to use the second arrow as the target point. Make your "impact board" entry in the corresponding second game frame.

In the next frame, enter the target line you will next attempt. When you have hit the pocket 3 times in a row with the correct target line (3 "17" entries in succession in the second gameline), or when you have completed 1 trial game, you may change to a new target line and trial game (see the Ten-to-Ten Line Example).

**Ten-to-Ten Line Example**

| Target line | 10 / 10 | 11 / 10 | 12 / 10 | 12 / 10 | 12 / 10 | | | | | |
|---|---|---|---|---|---|---|---|---|---|---|
| Impact point | 22 | 19 | 17 | 17 | 17 | | | | | |

b. *Moving to an Outside Target Point and Setup Location:* Next, change your target point to the first arrow (board number 5), and move your setup location 5 boards farther outside, so that you have a 5-to-5 target line. Record this change in the appropriate frame of the first gameline and continue to attempt to hit the pocket. Change your setup location if necessary, using the 3-0-1-2 system, until you hit the pocket. Continue to use the first arrow as your target point. Make your "impact board" entry in the corresponding second game frame.

In the next frame, enter the target line you will attempt. When you have hit the pocket 3 times in a row with the correct target line (3 "17" entries in succession in the frames of the second gameline), or when you have completed one trial game, you may change to a new target line (see the Adjustment to Outside Line Example).

**Adjustment to Outside Line Example**

| Target line | 5 / 5 | 4 / 5 | 3 / 5 | 3 / 5 | 3 / 5 | | | | | |
|---|---|---|---|---|---|---|---|---|---|---|
| Impact point | 12 | 15 | 17 | 17 | 17 | | | | | |

c. *Moving to an Inside Target Point and Setup Location:* Finally, change your target point to the third arrow (board number 15), and move your setup location further inside so that you now have a 15-to-15 target line. Record this change in the appropriate first gameline frame. Change your setup location if necessary, using the 3-0-1-2 system, until you hit the pocket. Continue to use the third arrow as the target point. Make your "impact board" entry in the corresponding second game frame.

In the next frame, enter the target line you will attempt. When you have hit the pocket 3 times in a row with the correct target line (3 "17" entries in succession in the frames of the second game line), or when you have completed 1 trial game, you may change to a new target line (see the Adjustment to Inside Line Example).

**Adjustment to Inside Line Example**

| Target line | 15 / 15 | 16 / 15 | 17 / 15 | 18 / 15 | 19 / 15 | 19 / 15 | 19 / 15 | | | |
|---|---|---|---|---|---|---|---|---|---|---|
| Impact point | 30 | 27 | 24 | 21 | 17 | 17 | 17 | | | |

**Success Goal** = Hit the pocket 3 times in a row, using 3 different target lines, or complete 5 trial games, whichever occurs first; use the following chart to keep track of your progress:

| Game number | Appropriate entry |
|:-----------:|:-----------------:|
| 1 | — |
| 2 | — |
| 3 | — |
| 4 | — |
| 5 | — |

(Entry: Enter "3PH" or a game score in the blanks.)

**Success Check**

- Roll 10 first balls ___
- Use a 10-to-10 target line ___
- Move to an outside target line ___
- Move to an inside target line ___

**To Increase Difficulty**

- When finished determining successful, pocket-hitting target lines, bowl 1 or more games, changing your target line each frame.

## 3. Target Swap

Learn to shoot different visual strike targets in an actual game situation, bowling against one or two opponents on the same lane. You should use a different visual target from your opponent while trying to outscore him or her. After each game, switch targets and bowl another competitive game. The objective is for all bowlers to use each of the 3 target points shown in Drill 2. (For example, TP #1 = 1st arrow, TP #2 = 2nd arrow, and TP #3 = 3rd arrow.)

**Success Goal** = Outscore your opponent, using 3 different target points (TP):

|  | Game 1 | | Game 2 | | Game 3 | |
|---|:---:|:---:|:---:|:---:|:---:|:---:|
|  | TP | Score | TP | Score | TP | Score |
| Your score | 1st | ___ | 2nd | ___ | 3rd | ___ |
| Opponent #1 | 1st | ___ | 2nd | ___ | 3rd | ___ |
| Opponent #2 | 1st | ___ | 2nd | ___ | 3rd | ___ |

**Success Check**

- Select target ___
- Take setup at appropriate location ___
- Roll a game using the target ___
- Switch targets ___

**To Increase Difficulty**

- Change your target line each frame.

**To Decrease Difficulty**

- Bowl two or three games using the same target line; then switch.

## 4. Rapid Target Line Adjustment

Combine your corrected strike-target line with slightly varied hand positions to learn how to change your target line in response to a new ball reaction.

Simulate an altered lane condition by deliberately changing your hand position to change the size of your hook. A slight change in hand position will not interfere with proper delivery technique. It is one of the acceptable variables that you may use to achieve different ball dynamics.

Prepare a scoresheet like the Sample Scoresheet, but wait to enter only the final, successful target line in the first frame of the first game space. Again, do not record second-ball attempts. Take your setup on the appropriate board for your successful strike-target line. If you must move, use the 3-0-1-2 system (see flowchart in Figure 8.1, p 114). Your partner will check to see whether you are executing properly. Note that this example assumes a Ten-to-Ten target line to start with; you'll use a different line from one hand position to another.

**Sample Scoresheet**

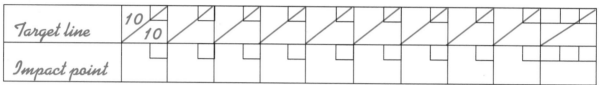

*First Hand Position:* Roll first balls until you hit your target line with a properly executed delivery. Use the 45-degree (moderate) hook-ball finger position (10 o'clock for right-handed bowlers, 2 o'clock for left-handers). As necessary, see Step 5 to review the clockface finger position terminology. Record data only if you are successful in hitting your target line and executing properly. You must be in agreement with your observer that your form was acceptable. Move your setup location if necessary until your ball is hitting the pocket. Record the impact board number in the corresponding second game frame and move on to the next frame.

*Second Hand Position:* When you have hit the pocket twice using the target line selected above, change your finger position to the vertical (more straightforward) position (12 o'clock for right-handers or left-handers). This position gives your ball more roll and, theoretically, less hook. Use the same target line and execute well, recording information only if you hit the target line. Move your setup location to accommodate the size of your new hook until your ball is once again hitting the pocket. Record your results.

*Third Hand Position:* When you have hit the pocket twice using the new target line, change your finger position to 90 degrees inside the vertical (9 o'clock for right-handers; 3 o'clock for left-handers), a position which gives more skid. Use the same target line and execute the delivery well, recording information only if you satisfy both requirements. Move your setup location to accommodate the size of your new hook until your ball is once again hitting the pocket. Record your results.

**Success Goal** = Hit the pocket 2 times using each of 3 different hand positions and accompanying target lines ___

### Success Check
- Bowl a 10-to-10 line to start ___
- Use moderate-hook hand position ___
- Move setup location if necessary ___
- Change to greater-roll hand position ___
- Move setup location if necessary ___
- Change to greater-skid hand position ___
- Move setup location if necessary ___

### To Increase Difficulty
- As soon as you have hit the pocket two times in a row with one hand position, change to another, move your setup location, and continue trying to hit the pocket.

## PHYSICAL ADAPTATIONS SUCCESS SUMMARY

It will take you a while to master appropriate adaptations to the common physical problems encountered in the bowling environment. Also, new situations will arise, further challenging your ability to adapt. As you encounter unusual physical conditions, review the eight common problems discussed in this step, and also review Figure 8.1 to evaluate your options. Remember that your response to these unusual conditions is under your control, once you are able to recognize how the various physical factors negatively effect your game. Then, you can select the most appropriate, safe (versus unsafe) adaptations to make in order to better manage your performance.

# STEP 9

# MENTAL DISCIPLINE: PRACTICING AND PLAYING SMART

A humorist once said, "You can't improve your aim by shooting at the moon." What he was saying is that you must have clearcut, attainable goals to be successful. The moon is too far away to hit, and you could not tell if you did hit it!

Goals and practice are natural partners; practice, whether mental or physical, must have definite outcomes, or goals. Otherwise, there is no reason to practice. Goal-oriented practice is, in itself, one of the most motivating aspects of bowling, because it is during practice that you can clearly see progress. Practice sessions are mirrors of your success, providing frequent opportunities for you to see yourself accomplishing the short-range goals that lead to long-range improvements. *Goal setting* is identifying a specific need or objective for the purpose of attaining it; it usually involves an action statement of the goal in clear, unambiguous terms. For a goal to be effective in modifying behavior, it should have to be accomplished within a time limit or within a given set of attempts. Good examples of goals in this book are the Keys to Success and the Success Check sections (listing technique or behaviors) and the Success Goal sections (identifying short-range performance).

Until now your focus has been on the physical skills of bowling. You have learned how to maintain physical control of your form through *kinesthetic sense* (feel) and how to modify your movement plan thoughtfully in response to different lane conditions. Now you have an opportunity to learn valuable mental skills and to combine these skills into a winning strategy for practicing and playing smart. You can use mental discipline—the use of your mind in productive ways—to deal effectively with potential interference with your concentration when you want to bowl your best.

## Why Is Mental Discipline Important?

Good bowling is nothing more than making the best shot that you can and correcting any errors on your very next shot. It is a program of constant troubleshooting and maintenance; it requires intense and constant concentration. Unless you can sustain concentration for extended periods of time, ever-present stressors will always bother you consciously and unconsciously, interfering with execution of your delivery and lowering your scores. Stressors cause excessive muscular tension, making your movements tentative and altering the timing relationships of body parts during your delivery. Applied leverage and the direction of your ball path usually become inconsistent.

Proper use of mental skills will help you perform better by enhancing concentration during practice and making you more resistant to pressure during competition. The better your mental skills, the more satisfaction you will derive from all types of bowling. You will "keep your head in the game" and take positive action—solving problems, making correct adjustments in playing lanes, monitoring execution, and so on. You will be taking charge of your performance rather than passively or negatively reacting to the environment. Even though you may not aspire to be a professional bowler, it is vital to your progress, if you pursue bowling as a meaningful activity, that you learn how to apply mental skills early in your development.

## Why Is Goal-Oriented Practice Important?

Although practice alone does not guarantee improvement, you can be assured that performance will not improve without it. Intelligent practice is goal-oriented practice. Through appropriate goal setting and practicing of attainable goals, you take control of your own development, becoming more self-reliant, gaining confidence in your ability, and cultivating a healthy attitude toward the sport. If you practice correctly (reaching reasonable goals) your performance will improve; if you practice incorrectly, either without goals or with unreasonable goals, your performance will worsen.

Improvement in performance will probably not occur at a consistent, steady pace. Your progress will be marked by performance level *plateaus*, during which you may experience little improvement or even a lowering of your scores. Plateaus are not all bad, however; they may indicate that new movement patterns are being integrated within your neuromuscular system and becoming automatic. Be patient with yourself and practice intelligently; you will see progress!

## How to Set Goals

For goals to be effective in directing your behavior toward their attainment, they must satisfy certain requirements. First, goals should be challenging but realistically attainable, that is, reasonable. Goals should be stated or set in such a manner that builds in probable success. You may adjust your goals down (make them easier) if necessary, or up (make them more difficult) at an appropriate time in your training. It is more beneficial to your progress to be successful in reaching easy goals than to fail at reaching difficult ones. Little victories build your confidence, helping you to think of yourself as a winner—even before you have actually won in competition.

Second, *performance goals* are more effective in improving skill than *outcome goals*. A performance goal involves the quality of execution or some intermediate accomplishment. For example, getting two strikes within five frames is a performance goal; five frames are under your direct control and the goal has built-in success. Winning a tournament, however, is an outcome goal; it is not completely under your direct control. Performance-oriented players—those who set performance goals—are more successful in attaining their goals than outcome-oriented players. Outcome-oriented players usually do not attain their goals, because outcome goals are loaded with built-in frustration. If you set your sights on good performance, though, satisfaction and a feeling of achievement are frequent, helping you improve rapidly. The following chart summarizes the characteristics of these two types of players:

### Performance-oriented player

Sets performance goals
Concerned with execution
Goals within control
Handles pressure well
More motivated
Eager goal-setter
Often successful
Judges self in terms of own successes

### Outcome-oriented player

Sets outcome goals
Concerned with winning
Goals beyond control
Too anxious under pressure
Less motivated
May reject goal setting
Less often successful
Judges self in terms of peer comparisons

Finally, you should set only positive goals in an active voice. For example, statements such as "I will make my next three spares," or "I can align properly to hit the pocket" are more specific, encouraging, and attainable than "I will not miss spares," or "I will not miss the pocket today."

### Short-Range Goals

You should use *short-range goals* as "stepping stones" to the attainment of *long-range goals*. For instance, the probability is very low that someone who has never piloted a plane before can take off, fly, and safely land on the first attempt. However, if that person is instructed in the first technique involved in flying, then the second, then the third, and so on, the probability of making a safe, successful solo flight increases greatly.

### Long-Range Goals

A long-range goal such as bowling a 300 game requires a series of short-range goals, each one being to get a strike. Each short-range goal of getting a strike itself requires other short-range goals leading to its attainment: executing the setup, the approach, and the release properly. Proper execution leads to strikes; strikes lead to 300 games. Specific goals and strategies are needed for attainment of a specific goal. Any specific goal is more effective in bringing about improvement than is a general, nonspecific one, like doing one's best or bowling well in a certain week.

### Goal-Setting Procedures

The following orderly sequence of suggestions will help you develop effective goals and strategies:

1. Develop a clear idea of what you want to achieve. Prioritize your desires, asking yourself, "How important is this desire in relation to the others?" Then write down each goal on a separate piece of paper or a notecard, leaving space underneath for listing strategies leading to attainment of the goal.

2. Decide how you will attain your goals. Under each goal, write action statements that clearly indicate the strategies that will accomplish it. List the strategies in the order in which they should occur, and leave some space between them. You may use either of two formats in formulating a goal:

   (a) subject + action verb + object ("I will pick up my next three spares"), or

   (b) "to" + action verb + object ("to make my next three spares").

3. Decide how you will carry out each goal-directed strategy. List these tactics in order (prioritize them) as well, and leave space between them.

4. Regularly compare your performance with your original, stated goals. Carry your list of goals and strategies with you so that you can read them often. Always know how you are progressing; such evaluation is absolutely necessary to promoting your continued effort and ultimate success. It's encouraging—every time you realize that you reach a goal, you can tell yourself that you are a success!

5. Provide yourself with a means of moral support. Associate only with positive-thinking persons who share your feelings about performance goals. You will have a difficult time applying yourself to the achievement of your goals if the "significant others" in your environment are not supportive, or if they are outcome oriented. Associate with successful persons, and you will have a better chance of becoming a success!

## Types of Physical Practice

There are three types of physical practice: *unsupervised*, or solo, practice; *reciprocal*, or *buddy-system*, practice; and *supervised* practice.

*Unsupervised practice* is carried out by you alone, without feedback from any source other than from your internal feelings, your kinesthetic sense, and other self-observations, as well as from the results at the pins. Unsupervised practice is particularly important when you are learning new movements requiring thoughtful repetition. To train your neuromuscular system, you must be able to isolate yourself from distractions and concentrate deeply, focusing your thoughts on a specific body part's position or action.

In *reciprocal (buddy-system) practice*, you are the performer and a partner is your observer; then the roles are switched so you can help each other. Verbal feedback from the observer is the special added element. Although you and your buddy need not be of equal proficiency in bowling, it is beneficial if you share a common goal of desired improvement, and have similar observation and concentration skills. Reciprocal practice is important because it provides you with accurate, instantaneous feedback from the observer. This timely feedback is very important so the feel associated with a given shot (which dissipates rapidly) is still fresh in your mind and muscles. Capturing this feel with the help of the observer's verbal feedback, along with the visual feedback of seeing how the pins act, adds greatly to your ability to *shape* (purposefully modify) your performance. It is vital that the observer not be distracted from observing consistently. The observer should not give feedback without actually having paid attention to the shot; the absence of feedback is better than inaccurate feedback.

In *supervised practice*, you are evaluated by a skilled, experienced bowler, and some type of instruction is usually given. Therefore, supervised practice usually involves the services of someone more highly trained than your buddy-system observer, such as an instructor or a coach. Traditional one-on-one bowling instruction falls into this category. A high-quality supervised practice session is very beneficial because it focuses on the bowling fundamentals. Your instructor can rebuild your game on these sound basics, one part at a time. Such instruction is most effective if each session presents you with no more than three new elements to practice. Trained supervision is beneficial when you want to bowl better but do not know how to do so. The goal should not be just to remove flaws from your technique, but to replace bad habits with good habits! It is best not to take instruction immediately before an important performance. The best time to restructure your technique is during the summer, a time when you may forsake league and tournament competition for learning.

# How to Practice

There are three parts to a good practice session: pre-practice preparations, conducting practice, and post-practice follow-up.

## Pre-Practice Preparations

Give yourself a good opportunity to make progress in practice by taking control of your situation. Try to ensure the following:

1. Pick a remote lane on which to bowl. If you are practicing your physical game, remove yourself from as many distractions as possible. Avoid eye contact with spectators; focus on yourself and what you want to accomplish. If you are working on your mental skills, you may actually want to challenge your ability to concentrate by bowling next to a noisy group.

2. If you must bowl a great number of games in a short period of time, bowl on an hourly-rate basis. If you need to practice slowly and deliberately, bowl on a per-game basis.

3. Do not keep a standard numerical score. The quality of your technique cannot be directly determined from your score, which is frequently a poor indicator of progress. If your score is kept by some sort of automatic scoring device, do not pay attention to it. You may keep some sort of score on paper, however, if directed to do so in one of the drills in this book.

4. Know precisely what you want to practice. Have it written down in the form of a performance-oriented goal, with strategies leading to its attainment. If you are using the buddy system to practice, both of you should receive instruction at the same time from the same instructor.

5. Always take some type of warm-up, preferably within five minutes of beginning to bowl. Warm-ups are essential in any sport because they help prepare you mentally as well as physically.

## Conducting Practice

Structure your practice session in accordance with the following suggestions. This procedure applies to both unsupervised and supervised practice. Do not engage in idle conversation until you reach the final point.

1. Take 5 to 10 shots to attain the proper feel before attempting to align yourself for a strike. If you are not executing your shot properly (i.e., if you do not feel unhurried, in rhythm, and unforced), trying to line up for your first-ball shot is useless.

2. Align yourself for your strike ball. Only when you are hitting your target line consistently can you truly fine-tune your delivery.

3. Begin to work on your goal. Your goal may be to complete one or more of the solo drills in this book; if so, follow all directions very closely. If your goal is general refinement of technique, concentrate on making a flowing motion, with proper execution on every shot. If your goal is improvement of a facet of your game (like poor hand position, torso instability, bending your knees at the wrong moment, etc.), focus your selective attention strongly on only the body parts involved. Always note what effects varying an execution facet has on your ball's path, a good source of feedback. Note that a change to better technique usually increases your leverage, requiring you to realign your strike target line.

4. Write down all important, useful information in your notes. If you are using the buddy system, include your observer's feedback. Log any and all indications of progress, no matter whether objective or subjective. Such entries in your notes represent small, but clear victories that build your confidence, helping to make your attitude toward practice more positive and your outlook on your entire game more optimistic. Use these notes to revise your list of performance-oriented goals.

5. End the practice session when appropriate. If you are performing well and are not tired, try to continue bowling as long as you can, to further refine the correct movements. If you must quit but are not tired, make a few more of the correct movements to ingrain them before you stop, quitting on the upswing. When you are tired, stop practicing. When you are performing poorly for any reason and cannot seem to make the correct movements, stop! Do not allow yourself to practice poor performance!

If you are using the buddy system, the time to switch roles is when the performer is tired, allowing him or her to rest and observe the other member of the buddy team. It is best not to switch roles until the performer has deeply sensed the results of a properly executed shot; it should be locked into the mind and muscles before he or she stops.

## Post-Practice Follow-Up

Once you stop bowling, consider the following suggestions:

1. Put away your equipment properly and use a cool-down. Relax for a short period before beginning a new activity.

2. Take your notes home and think about them. Resolve what needs to be done prior to your next practice session; for instance, you may need to improve your ball fit, buy a new pair of shoes, review your target lines, or update your short-term and/or long-term goals to be reasonable, positive, and performance oriented.

# Mental Discipline

You can improve your concentration by developing three important mental skills: anxiety reduction,

positive self-statements, and mental imagery (or mental practice).

## Anxiety Reduction

The first mental skill you should use faithfully is anxiety reduction to help control any nervousness. Three elements are involved in reducing anxiety:

1. Become aware of all factors that produce muscular tension and other forms of stress in you. Be honest in your self-evaluation. Write down as many specific upsetting persons, events, negative thoughts, and situations as possible. Have a frequent bowling partner help you discover more; others can see you reacting negatively (through your *body language* and other cues) even when you are not aware of your reaction.

2. Apply a *progressive relaxation* technique. When you develop skill in relaxation, you become aware of muscular tension as it develops. You will then be able to relax your muscles at will.

3. Combine progressive muscle relaxation with specific stressors. This process, called *coping*, will deactivate your tension-producing response to these stressors. A useful technique is to make an audio tape in which you briefly present each stressful situation to yourself in your own voice. Each presentation can be followed by a pause to allow you to consciously relax any muscles that may be tensing. If you repeat this procedure often enough, you will relax automatically when the stressful situations occur in real life.

## Positive Self-Statements

A second mental skill you should use all the time is *making positive self-statements*. You should make a list of short statements about yourself and your performance, positive in tone, to repeat to yourself *(self-talk)* during competition. Never say anything negative or demeaning to yourself; always encourage yourself. These positive ideas will replace and exclude any negative thoughts.

## Mental Practice

A third mental skill you should use is *mental imagery*, also known as *mental practice* or *mental rehearsal*. Mental practice involves creating an ideal experience in your "mind's eye"—you picture yourself taking your setup and approach, and delivering your ball to achieve a perfect result. The imaging process actually organizes your muscles to respond correctly, by imprinting a performance standard in your neuromuscular system.

By using mental practice, you effectively run your movement plan without actually bowling. If you use mental practice on a regular basis, you can program proper technique and correct problems and mistakes instead of hoping that such things will work themselves out—which they will not! Many top sport stars make consistent use of imagery to maintain superior performance. You may use imagery to help ingrain smooth and flawless bowling movements into your performance techniques.

If you cannot afford to practice physically as often as you like, or if a bowling center is not conveniently located, you may want to carry out mental practice at regular intervals. This is not to suggest that you can train yourself effectively with no actual physical practice, but you can make faster progress if you regularly use both methods.

If your physical performance is flawed with poor equipment or technique, your movement plan cannot run properly, and there is no point in trying to attain mental control over it! Your subconscious mind cannot be convinced that you are prepared. You may be tempted to blame a lack of some mental skill, such as concentration, for a bad shot, when it was really caused by a loose thumbhole or a badly worn sliding sole. Ensure that your bowling ball and shoes fit well so that they are not technique-interfering. Also, drill extensively on the correct movements; *overlearn* them until you have complete confidence in your ability to perform well-executed shots. Be physically ready first, be mentally ready next, and win!

## How to Organize and Incorporate Mental Skills

The best and most successful professional bowlers seem to be in a "trance" when they are in competition. They may or may not be cordial, and they seem to shun unnecessary contact in favor of staying focused. Just look into the eyes of Walter Ray Williams, Jr. when he is "in the hunt" on the Professional Bowlers Tour television program. His mind is focused and his aim is deadly!

Figure 9.1 shows an effective preshot or Mental Toughness Routine that begins long before you roll your first ball. It remains in force continuously until after you have rolled your last ball. The objective of this organized routine of mental discipline is to keep your attention steadily focused on tasks beneficial to your performance and away from thoughts of failure; it keeps your mind productive and not destructive.

Because a Mental Toughness Routine requires relative silence and isolation, it may appear to be a way to intimidate an opponent; however, it is neither arrogance nor unfriendliness. It is simply a way of creating and maintaining a proper environment for sustained concentration during competition, and must involve the following disciplines:

- Maintaining mental control during and between games.
- Talking only if it is absolutely necessary; do not initiate or cultivate conversation, and do not encourage eye contact.
- *Never* watching anyone bowl. To do so could interfere with your own movement plan, for example, make you speed up your approach or muscle the ball because the person you are watching is doing so!

The Mental Toughness Routine, as depicted in Figure 9.1, is organized into the following phases:

**Relief Time:** The preshot portion of your routine takes place in the period of time between shots (usually 2 to 5 minutes) as well as the period between games of a bowling session. Spend this time wisely, using it to plan physical adjustments to lane conditions, to make modifications to your bowling ball, and so on. Sit down and stay calm, isolating yourself from potential interferences. You may assist in keeping score and talk when necessary during relief time, but do not engage in idle conversation.

If you are a doubles or a team player, use limited conversation—only to encourage or help a teammate as necessary. Simply confine such talk to your relief time. If you are having difficulty, your teammates will understand if you isolate yourself from them for additional mental imagery and planning during your relief time.

**Mental Planning:** Remain seated and focus your thoughts deeply, spending at least 20 seconds preparing yourself before standing up for your next shot (before spare balls or between shots in the 10th frame,

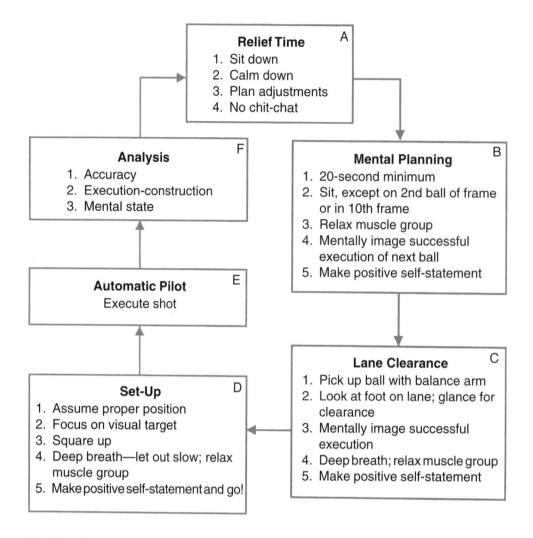

**Figure 9.1** Mental toughness routine flowchart.

*Note*: Derived from the ideas of W. Powers, personal communication, May, 1987.

you do not have to sit down). During this time, do not keep score or engage in any conversation.

Consciously relax your muscles and conduct mental imagery and positive self-talk. If you are having a problem achieving good concentration, or if you are bowling on a particularly difficult lane condition, you may expand the mental planning phase to fill the entire time between shots, effectively replacing your relief time. Be aware, however, that you can become mentally fatigued if you do not give yourself sufficient relief time for tension reduction.

**Lane Clearance:** Take the next-up position, holding your ball in your balance arm to minimize strain on your bowling arm. Look at your intended setup location on the approach while you make either different or the same positive self-statements you made during the mental planning phase. Do not let your eyes dwell on the other bowlers. Simply image yourself properly executing the shot (while you simply glance for clearance on either side).

**Setup:** Right before you initiate movement, add a deep, relaxing breath to your usual setup routine. Make a last positive self-statement and immediately initiate movement.

**Automatic Pilot Execution:** During practice it may be necessary to focus your attention on your hand, your foot, or the timing between body parts, as you have done in previous drills. However, during competition, the fewer things you monitor consciously, the better.

On each shot, always be mindful of your cadence, the coordination between your pushaway and your first step, and the destination of your pushaway, while your gaze is fixed on your visual target. During competition, you should generally be on automatic pilot. However, in the case of unpredictable lane conditions or slippery or sticky approaches, you may have to carry out additional conscious monitoring of your body parts to ensure some consistency (or even your physical safety).

*Analysis:* Immediately after you have made your shot, objectively analyze it for accuracy, quality of execution, and your mental state. Because performers tend to be very critical of themselves after a poor shot, keeping the mind busy with objective analysis helps to exclude negative feelings. You must be *very analytical for a short period of time.* Then you should enter the relief-time phase, using the analysis information and deciding on the strategy for your next shot. Quickly clear your mind and enter the mental planning phase.

## MENTAL DISCIPLINE SUCCESS STOPPERS

Your ability to organize your actions into purposeful practice and game play is critical to your bowling success. Look for three potential areas where you may be making errors: goal setting, physical practice, and mental discipline. Although negative feelings in themselves are not mistakes, not dealing quickly and effectively with negative feelings and behaviors when they occur are themselves errors in behavior. Resulting interruptions in concentration and muscular control will cause performance errors. It is often difficult, however, to link specific execution errors (e.g., a tentative balance arm) with the omission of a particular element from the routine (e.g., no positive self-statement). If you can recognize some of the feelings and behaviors that accompany ineffective mental discipline management during your performance, you can identify deviations from your routine and take quick corrective action before problems become more complex. Common errors and how to correct them follow.

| Error | Correction |
| --- | --- |
| *Goal Setting* | |
| 1. Failing to reach difficult goals. | 1. Break the difficult goal down into smaller goals you can achieve on the way to the difficult one. |
| 2. Trying to attain an outcome goal, such as "to bowl a 300 this game." | 2. Set a realistic performance goal for yourself. It will help you achieve the *outcome* as a result of attaining the *performance* goal. |
| 3. Trying to reach a nonspecific goal, such as "I will bowl well." | 3. Develop a clear idea of what you want to achieve first. |
| 4. Losing track of your progress; lacking motivation. | 4. Regularly compare your performance with your original, stated goals. Associate only with positive-thinking persons who share your feelings about performance goals. |

| Error | Correction |
|---|---|
| ***Physical Practice*** | |
| 1. Attempting serious practice when being distracted. | 1. Pick a remote lane on which to bowl. |
| 2. Being conscious of the score during practice. | 2. Do not keep a standard numerical score. If your score is kept by some sort of automatic scoring device, do not pay attention to it. |
| 3. Practicing without purpose—just "rolling balls." | 3. Know precisely what you want to practice and how you intend to do so. |
| 4. Not remembering what you did during practice. | 4. Write down all important, useful information in your notes. |
| 5. Being tired and uncoordinated during practice. | 5. When you are tired, stop practicing. Do not practice poor performance! |
| ***Mental Discipline*** | |
| 1. You lost coordination but do not know why. | 1. Check and correct the quality of your pushaway, and the coordination between your pushaway and first step. Refine your post-shot analysis and run your mental imagery more often during relief time. Do not watch anyone else bowl. |
| 2. During competition, you catch yourself idly watching others bowl. | 2. Isolate yourself more deeply; close your eyes, if necessary. |
| 3. You feel resentful or angry during competition. | 3. Increase the frequency of positive self-statements in your routine. |
| 4. You feel that you cannot win or that you want to give up. | 4. Relax your muscles, isolate yourself more deeply, refine your post-shot analysis, and increase the frequency of "I can" positive self-statements. |
| 5. You feel hyped, catch yourself gritting your teeth, or develop a headache. | 5. Increase the frequency of muscle-relaxation periods in your routine. |
| 6. You feel lost or unable to concentrate. | 6. Isolate yourself more deeply, close your eyes, and try to see more detail in your mental image. |
| 7. You are unable to remember what you did on your last shot. | 7. Refine your self-analysis skills. Start analyzing as soon as the ball is on its way down the lane. As you walk back from the foul line, ask yourself, "What did I do wrong (or right) on this shot?" Plan your next shot based upon your answer, and mentally image yourself executing the next shot correctly to clarify your expectations, so that you can better identify your actions after the actual shot. |
| 8. You are unable to visualize yourself performing a perfect shot in detail. | 8. Refine your mental imagery skills through additional mental practice. |

**MENTAL DISCIPLINE**

# DRILLS

## *1. Goal Development*

Pick one or more goals from the following "Sample List of Ultimate Goals," and write this goal down on a piece of paper. Under your ultimate goal statement, write the short-range goals and strategies you will use to attain your ultimate goal. You may draw flowcharts to help you visualize how the goals and strategies relate to each other (see the following flowchart example). When you are through, check your goals against the criteria presented in the text, and record them in the space provided.

### Sample List of Ultimate Goals

a. Practice
- To make 10 pocket hits in a game
- To be on balance at the foul line 8 times out of 10
- To recite the series of checks in the setup from Step 1
- To develop a strong game

b. Competition
- To win
- To win money
- To win a tournament
- To average 200
- To shoot an all-spare game
- To have an above-average performance

c. Team
- To become a supportive teammate
- To have the highest average on the team
- To bowl leadoff position on the team

d. League
- To gain greater enjoyment from league competition
- To help the league run more smoothly
- To become a league officer

*Flowchart Example*: Start with an ultimate goal and work backward to determine what short-range goals are necessary in working toward it. Work backward from each short-range goal to develop strategies to attain it. Your flowchart may also be branched, with several goals not related to each other leading to the attainment of a single, ultimate goal. Many goal heirarchies are possible (see Figure 9.2, a-c).

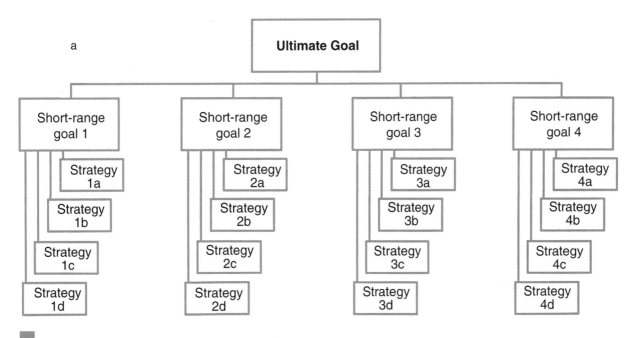

**Figure 9.2** Three different types of flowcharts for goal setting: (a) ladder format, (b) pyramid format, and (c) formula format.

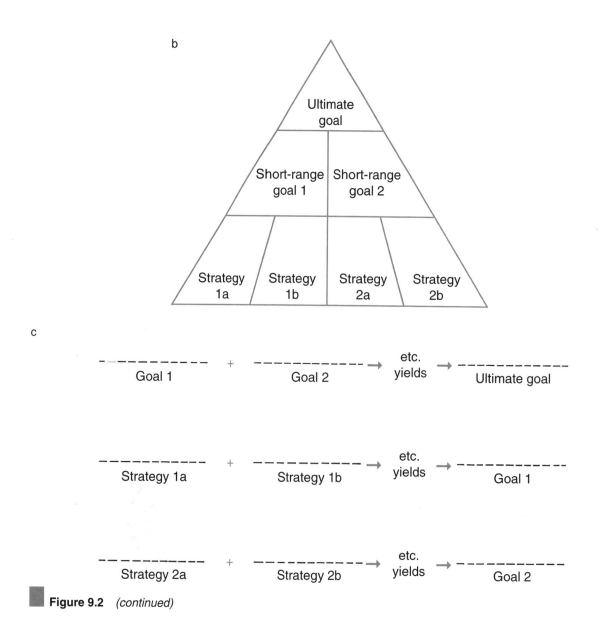

**Figure 9.2** *(continued)*

**Success Goal** = Develop at least two ultimate goals __

**a. Ultimate goal** _____

   *Goal 1* _____

   *Strategy 1a* _____

   *Strategy 1b* _____

   **Goal 2** _____

   *Strategy 2a* _____

   *Strategy 2b* _____

**b. Ultimate goal** _____

   *Goal 1* _____

   *Strategy 1a* _____

   *Strategy 1b* _____

   **Goal 2** _____

   *Strategy 2a* _____

   *Strategy 2b* _____

**Success Check**
- Write down ultimate goal ___
- Write down short-range goals ___
- Write down short-range strategies ___
- Discuss your goals ___

**Example**

**Ultimate goal**: I will bowl 20 pins higher in the next game.

**Goal 1**: I will hit the headpin more often.

*Strategy 1a*: I will make the appropriate adjustment in the setup.

*Strategy 1b*: I will concentrate more effectively on the shot.

**Goal 2**: I will make one more strike.

*Strategy 1a*: I will setup more carefully.

*Strategy 1b*: I will focus more intensely on the target.

**To Increase Difficulty**
- Chart your progress over several practice sessions, then modify your strategies as necessary to meet your goals.

**To Decrease Difficulty**
- Discuss your goals with a partner or instructor as you develop them.

## 2. Charting Progress: Unsupervised Practice

This drill shows you how to use a scoresheet to record your performance when practicing alone. Obtain a regular scoresheet. If your score is kept by an automatic scoring device, make a scoresheet for yourself. Do not keep score in the conventional manner; rather, you should record the following types of information (the examples are for a right-handed bowler):

a. *Type of strike*: As the game progresses, write "P" for a solid pocket hit, "M" for a light mixer or shaker (a pocket hit in which the headpin rebounds off the side wall or kickboard), "4" for a slow 4-pin topple, "W" for a "weak 10" hit (the 10 pin barely topples), "B" for a Brooklyn hit, and so on in the appropriate frame spaces.

b. *Pins left standing*: List them from the lowest to the highest number—the 2-4-5, or the *bucket* (2-4-5-8), or a *washout* (1-2-4-10), and so on.

c. *Ball used during the game*: Describe this in the left half of the gameline space reserved for your name.

d. *Line played*: Use the right half of the name space to indicate the target line you are playing during the game, such as 13-10 or 12-11.

e. *Write anything else of value (below the respective frame)*: How you felt, whether you pulled the ball, and so on.

A game annotated in this fashion may look like the Sample Self-Scorecard. The results of your shots are recorded within the frame boxes, while comments regarding your performance are written below the respective boxes. You can learn something about the quality of your approach and delivery in each frame by studying your notations. Such scoresheets may be especially useful in helping to determine skills that need extra attention.

**Sample Self-Scorecard**

**Success Goal** = Complete and score one unsupervised practice game as directed above ___

**Success Check**
- Bowl practice games by yourself ___
- Make performance notations on scoresheet ___
- Analyze the notations on the scoresheet ___

## 3. Charting Progress: Practice With Observer Feedback

This drill shows you how to use a scoresheet to record your performance when practicing while being observed by a partner (buddy), an instructor, or a coach. Your observer should prepare the scoresheet and make entries as directed in the previous drill, recording only information relevant to your execution and pinfall results. Your observer should write down information such as:

1. type of strike
2. pins left standing
3. ball used during the game, and
4. line played, as well as that which you could not be expected to know, including:
   - the actual path that the ball followed; this will not always be the same as the target line (the line played) you elected to use at the start of the game;
   - early, late, or in-time pushaway;
   - early, late, or in-time ball at the release;
   - bending over too far at the waist; and
   - any other relevant information that only an observer can see.

In the Sample Observer Scorecard, the results of your shots are recorded in the frame boxes, while the observer's comments are written below the respective boxes. Such scoresheets help you give attention to skills that you may neglect because it is difficult to detect them on your own.

**Sample Observer Scorecard**

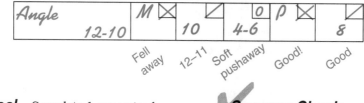

**Success Goal** = Complete 1 supervised practice game ___

**Success Check**
- Bowl practice games with observer ___
- Observer makes performance notations on scoresheet ___
- Discuss notations on both scoresheets ___

## 4. Willful Relaxation

Anxiety reduction means willful relaxation in response to stressful situations. An extreme example of a stressful situation is having nine strikes in a row and having to wait to bowl your tenth frame for a 300 game. You can use this drill to learn how to reduce your anxiety in game situations. This exercise is based on the well-accepted Jacobson Progressive Relaxation Technique of 1930. The advantage of this technique is an increased awareness of the contrast between tension and lack of tension. Set aside about 30 minutes for your initial attempts of this drill. As you become more familiar with the technique, you can shorten the time.

*Directions for Practice*: Sit down or lie down and relax. Close your eyes and inhale as deeply as possible; exhale slowly and completely. Feel your body becoming more and more relaxed. Continue taking in and expelling air in the same manner.

Start systematically relaxing each muscle group in your body from the feet and moving up to your head and face. For example, first extend and then flex the muscles of your left foot, holding the tension in the flexed position for 10 seconds. Take a deep breath and let it out slowly as you let the muscles relax. Stay relaxed and quiet for 20 seconds. Move on to the next muscle group.

Use a systematic order, such as the following list, for alternating tensing and progressively relaxing each muscle group.

| | | | | | |
|---|---|---|---|---|---|
| Left foot | → | Right foot | Left triceps | → | Right triceps |
| Left calf | → | Right calf | Abdominal group | | |
| Left quad | → | Right quad | Pectorals | | |
| Left hamstring | → | Right hamstring | Back and shoulders | | |
| Left hand | → | Right hand | Neck | | |
| Left forearm | → | Right forearm | Face | | |
| Left biceps | → | Right biceps | | | |

When you have completed the list of muscle groups, lay relaxed for a few minutes. In this relaxed state, you are most receptive to suggestion, so use the time for other types of rehearsal, such as mental bowling practice or making positive self-affirmation statements. Avoid dropping off to sleep until you are finished rehearsing.

*During Competition*: You do not usually have time to lie down, so you must relax while sitting down between shots during a game. Identify the most tense muscle group (usually the jaw and/or the neck and shoulders), and, while sitting tall in your chair, close your eyes and inhale as deeply as possible; exhale slowly and completely. Try to "run" your relaxation routine as quickly as possible, starting with your feet and moving up to your head and face. Be sure to relax your jaw, neck, and shoulders if you do not have time to relax anything else.

**Success Goal** = Complete the list above, relaxing each muscle group completely; try to completely relax all your muscles in a shorter period each time ___

**Success Check**
• Choose a peaceful setting ___
• Breathe deeply; exhale slowly ___
• Progressively relax your muscle groups ___
• Use the relaxed state for other types of rehearsal ___

**To Increase Difficulty**
• Put yourself in a stressful situation, such as a crowded bowling center, or in a highly competitive situation, such as a tournament, and try to relax progressively.

**To Decrease Difficulty**
• In a soft voice, record your preferred progressive relaxation routine, including self-affirmation statements such as "I will feel calm and alert." Consider adding soothing background music, and listen to it daily.

## 5. Self-Affirmations

Self-affirmation is saying positive, motivational statements to yourself. It is a form of rehearsal that is appropriate anytime, anywhere. Just like mental practice, it is easiest in a peaceful setting and best done right after completing the progressive relaxation technique. However, positive self-talk is useful during competition in the bowling center, so it is beneficial to "talk to yourself" between, and just before, shots.

Some examples of positive self-talk are:

- "I will make a good shot."
- "I am very relaxed."
- "Good shot."
- "Better shot next time."

As you see, these statements may be only two or three words long, and they are always positive. Just like performance goals, *they never involve outcomes*, such as getting a strike, winning the tournament, and so on; they are motivational and should never call attention to "things that can go wrong."

Write several positive self-statements that mean something to you and that you can use during practice and competition. Then bowl three games making these statements to yourself between and/or directly before each shot. Record your use of them below.

**Success Goal** = Complete a 3-game series using positive self-talk before each shot (figure an average of approximately 18 shots per game; one shot for a frame with a strike, two shots for a frame with a spare); use the chart below to keep track of the number of times per game you used a positive self-statement:

| Game 1 | Game 2 | Game 3 |
| --- | --- | --- |
| ＿＿ | ＿＿ | ＿＿ |

**Success Check**

- Write down positive self-statements ＿
- Bowl 3 games ＿
- Use positive self-talk between and just before each shot ＿

**To Increase Difficulty**

- Put yourself in a stressful situation, such as a crowded bowling center, or in a highly competitive situation, such as a tournament, and try to use positive self-talk.

**To Decrease Difficulty**

- If you are having difficulty identifying some positive self-affirmations, ask other bowlers what types they find helpful to use and when they use them.

## 6. Mental Practice

Mental practice will help you improve! You may conduct mental practice anytime or anywhere. It is easiest in a peaceful setting while you are lying down. You may mentally "bowl" three games before you go to sleep. Better yet, you can conduct mental practice after completing the progressive relaxation technique. You may also mentally bowl a game during a rest break in the bowling center, but it is more difficult, due to visual distraction and noise. Do *not* allow yourself to fall asleep until you have finished mental practice.

*Directions for Practice*: Sit down or lie down and relax. Close your eyes and inhale as deeply as possible; exhale slowly and completely. Feel your body becoming more and more relaxed. Continue taking in and expelling air in the same manner.

Just as if you were running a film in your mind, close your eyes and watch yourself take your setup and make only deliveries that result in success, that is, making strikes or spares (never "see" yourself leaving a spare on a strike attempt). Repeat these mental shots over and over, bowling a 3-game series. *Note*: If you're having difficulty seeing yourself, watch a videotape of yourself using proper execution. Then turn the tape off and replay in your mind what you saw.

**Success Goal** = Complete a 3-game series of mental practice ___

**Success Check**
- Choose a peaceful setting ___
- Relax ___
- Watch yourself bowl in your mind's eye ___

### To Increase Difficulty
- Conduct mental practice sitting up in the bowling center.
- Keep score either mentally, or on a notepad.

### To Decrease Difficulty
- Review your best game's scoresheet, then mentally practice what you did to achieve such a good game.

## 7. Mental Toughness Routine Quiz

This drill will help you understand the Mental Toughness Routine. Review the Mental Toughness Routine shown in Figure 9.1 and the explanation given. Note the sequence of events and time relationships indicated in the text. When you feel ready, answer the following questions.

### Questions

a. During what phase should you plan target line adjustments?
b. Between what phases does the Mental Planning phase occur?
c. What type of execution should you mentally image?
d. Under what circumstances may you talk during competition?
e. During what phase do you look down at your setup location?
f. During what phase do you look at your visual target?
g. During what phases is the use of positive self-statements suggested?
h. What three elements should you analyze immediately after a shot?
i. In a 3-game series, how many times may you break concentration?

**Success Goal** = Answer all 9 questions correctly ___

### To Increase Difficulty

• Answer the questions without referring to the flowchart or notes.

### To Decrease Difficulty

• Refer to the flowchart when necessary, and discuss the questions with a partner.

**Answer Key**

a. Relief time
b. Relief time and lane clearance
c. Successful only
d. Only if it is absolutely necessary
e. Lane clearance
f. Setup
g. Mental planning, lane clearance, and setup
h. Accuracy, execution, and mental state
i. None

## 8. Psychological Scorecard

This solo drill requires you to monitor the quality of your behavior and mental state for each shot of a 2-game series. Strictly follow the Mental Toughness Routine. Keep a standard numerical bowling score, but, in the corresponding frame of the gameline directly below the one on which you are keeping score, put one or more of the following abbreviations for the behaviors you show for each ball (see the Sample Scorecard).

**N** = negative thinking
**L** = lack of close attention
**O** = overexcited
**U** = under-motivated
**C** = complete mental control
**F** = failure to use routine

**Sample Scorecard**

| | | | | | | | | | | |
|---|---|---|---|---|---|---|---|---|---|---|
| Brandon | ⊠ | 7 2̸ | 8 ⟋ | ⊠ | 8 Ø | 9 ⟋ | ⊠ | ⊠ | 9 ⟋ | ⊠ 6 3 |
| | 17 | 26 | 46 | 66 | 85 | 105 | 134 | 154 | 174 | 193 |
| (Mental state) | L | FF | LC | C | LC | C | CL | LL | CC | CL U |

When you are finished, record your game scores below. Count the frequency of each abbreviation and insert the number opposite the abbreviation. The most frequent abbreviation indicates your most frequent behavior.

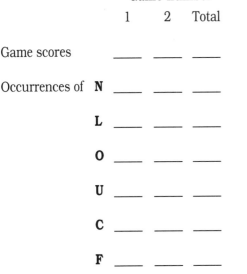

**Success Goal** = Use the chart below to keep track of the following criteria:

a. above-average scores in both games

b. less than 2 occurrences of each abbreviation other than C

c. 20 or more occurrences of abbreviation C

**Game number**

| | 1 | 2 | Total |
|---|---|---|---|
| Game scores | ___ | ___ | ___ |
| Occurrences of **N** | ___ | ___ | ___ |
| **L** | ___ | ___ | ___ |
| **O** | ___ | ___ | ___ |
| **U** | ___ | ___ | ___ |
| **C** | ___ | ___ | ___ |
| **F** | ___ | ___ | ___ |

**Success Check**
- Bowl 2 games ___
- Follow the Mental Toughness Routine (MTR) ___
- Record numerical score ___
- Record your mental state ___

**To Increase Difficulty**
- Bowl in actual competition, following the MTR and keeping track of the behaviors. You may use an observer to help identify and record behavior.

**To Decrease Difficulty**
- Use an observer to help you identify and record behavior.

## MENTAL DISCIPLINE SUCCESS SUMMARY

You may not see the benefits of mental discipline until you have put it into practice for a while. *The key is to continue to use the Mental Toughness Routine—even when it does not seem to be of benefit and when you seem to be the most frustrated with yourself.* Have your teacher, coach, or a trained observer qualitatively evaluate your mental discipline in practice, league, and tournaments, according to the procedures set forth in the drills. As necessary, ask your teacher, coach, or a trained observer to assist you in developing goals and charting progress for both practice and open bowling. Allow him or her to qualitatively evaluate your technique according to the procedures set forth in the drills; then practice smart!

# STEP 10

## LEAGUES AND TOURNAMENTS: COMPETING FOR SUCCESS

All through the decades, special bowlers have shown the ability to win in competition—Ned Day, Buddy Bomar, Billy Welu, Don Carter, Dick Weber, Earl Anthony, Marion Ladewig, Betty Morris, Patty Costello, Lisa Wagner, and others. The most successful bowlers are comfortable in competition, seemingly thriving on the pressure and able to win against heavy odds.

What this Step is all about is helping you be successful in competition. You cannot learn everything you need to know from a book; most competitive skills must be acquired and refined during years of actual competition. However, the lessons in this book will save you some time. By the end of this step, you'll be familiar with the common protocols used in match play, in medal play, or in combination scoring systems; use a scoring index to detect how far behind your team is from the opposing team; bowl Scotch doubles and best-ball doubles; identify ways to foster team spirit; know when to follow one-lane, two-lane, or one-pair courtesy rules; and understand two methods of determining handicaps.

## Why Is the Ability to Compete Successfully Important?

Competition is good for you; it is a natural step in your growth as a bowler and as an individual. To see how your performance "stacks up" against that of others can build your confidence and help you become an even better player. The best way to achieve the highest level of refinement in your game is through competition. Furthermore, if you learn how to be successful in a sport, you may apply the mechanics of success to many other life situations.

## How to Compete Successfully

If you choose to compete, always set your mind to be successful. You must know how to use all the skills and strategies you have already learned, and also be able to stay motivated while using additional strategies specific for competitive situations. If you are a team bowler, you have an additional obligation to help your teammates focus their minds on the common goal of making well-executed shots and to behave in a manner that will enhance performance. The following suggestions will help you.

*Between Competitive Sessions*: Be prepared! The objective of proper preparation is to remove any potential barriers to your success. Knowing that you are not prepared can shake your confidence; knowing that you *could* have prepared yourself, but neglected to do so, is more self-defeating. Give your self-image a break—be prepared and know that you are prepared!

1. Acquire relevant knowledge or an essential skill well in advance of competition. Give yourself plenty of time to understand a concept and develop skills through practice. Memorize that fact! Do that drill! Ingrain that movement through intense practice!
2. Put generous effort into preparing your equipment. Do not allow equipment discrepancies to become easy excuses for poor performance, setting yourself up for failure. Make that span correct! Make that thumbhole fit properly! Repair that worn area on your bowling shoe!
3. If you are not physically and mentally sharp, do not compete. Often the eagerness of a player to compete alters his or her judgment with

respect to potential performance likely to result from an incomplete state of preparation. Do not fall into this trap!

*At The Competition Site Prior to Competition:* When you arrive at the competition site, stay calm and try to get settled. You are cast into a new situation that presents many possibilities. Avoid continuous distraction by accomplishing the following:

1. Get organized. You must be sure that you have everything in order, so you are not preoccupied and your mind is free to concentrate on bowling. If possible, talk with someone ahead of time so you will know what to do to get settled. Be on time and respect your teammates, your opponents, and the host establishment. Know what you should do with your bowling equipment, know where and how to check in, know on what lanes you will bowl, know where you will store your personal items, and so on.

2. Complete any necessary preliminary paperwork before competition begins. Before taking any practice balls, and preferably before entering the settee area, take care of all fees, applications, entry blanks, and record-keeping. Do not allow paperwork to distract you or your teammates from good performance.

3. Devise a sensible plan for playing the lanes before you begin. Arrive early during a tournament to see how other players are playing the lanes. Try to observe the target lines of bowlers who roll the ball similarly to you. However, do not let your eyes dwell on the mechanics of their deliveries; watch only the dynamics of their balls on the lane surfaces. Write down the lane number, the line played, and the time of the day.

4. Close your ears to idle talk from other players. Although fellow players may not necessarily be trying to interfere with your thinking, idle talk is usually negative and misleading, and can affect your performance.

5. Take care of last-minute problems with your bowling equipment. Make a final check of the ball to see if you must clean or put tape in the thumbhole or change finger grips. Check the laces on your shoes to ensure that they will not break during competition. Make sure that you will have your accessories (tape, scissors, towel, etc.) with you when you go to your assigned lanes.

6. When you have "taken care of business" as described above, begin to focus on yourself and your performance. Begin your anxiety reduction, positive self-talk, and mental practice procedures. Always assume success!

*During Singles Competition:* As a singles competitor, you are all alone. You must think constantly and act quickly if you are to be successful. The following set of tactics should become part of your successful strategy:

1. Get lined up during your warm-up on your starting pair of lanes. Begin by using the same target line on each lane of the pair. Try your favorite target line first, then if you must adjust, use the 3-0-1-2 system. During your practice period, correct your list of strike-target lines with updated information on your starting pair of lanes.

2. During competition, be alert but calm, making strict use of your Mental Toughness Routine. Remember the previous shot and make quick, thoughtful corrections when necessary. Always keep trying, no matter how far behind you may seem to be.

3. In moving from one pair of lanes to another, have someone (partner, instructor, coach, etc.) look ahead to the pair to which you will move and write down the latest target-line information for each lane. Moving from pair to pair presents the possibility of your wasting four shots at the start of a game in attempting to get lined up, so good preparation is a must. If you cannot have someone look ahead, use the same target lines for the next pair as you are using on the current pair, then adjust systematically. Generally speaking, as a lane is bowled on, the oil dressing is displaced and the correct target line becomes more diagonal and toward the inside. For example, if you started with a 10-to-10 target line, after several games, the target line may have moved to 13-to-11 or even 16-to-13.

*During Team Competition:* Foster team spirit! A team can perform better if it is cohesive and united in the pursuit of its goals, and if its standard for productivity (bowling success) is high. You and your teammates can foster your team's spirit, keeping a winning attitude at all times, if you consistently do the following:

1. Promote team closeness and distinctiveness from the other teams. Arrange some leisure time together for the team, in addition to the usual bowling sessions. Wear team uniforms during league and tournament play.

2. Ensure similarity of goals. Ensure that each member of the team is in harmony with respect to attitudes, desires, level of commitment, and ability. Reliability is a very desirable characteristic. Members should attend regularly, pay their fees on time, and show concern for the welfare of the team. Balance in ability is a concern, because each member should feel that he or she is carrying a fair share of the load. Once your team is stabilized, try to minimize turnover.

3. Emphasize group goals and rewards. Recognize team excellence. Recognize individual excellence in the context of how it contributes to team excellence. Teamwork involves recognition of each other's accomplishments.

4. Before competition, while you are lining yourself up during practice, help your teammates line up and make a ball selection.

5. Make optimum use of your team lineup. You can increase your five-member team's chances of winning if you line up your bowlers as follows.

   a. First, or *leadoff*, bowler: your most consistent bowler. The teammates should pay attention to the leadoff bowler's line and "go to school" on the shots.

   b. Second bowler: a steady bowler and a good spare shooter. When selecting the first and second bowler, it is often helpful to cluster two bowlers who usually bowl doubles competition together to motivate each other.

   c. Third bowler: generally the least consistent team member or the one with the lowest average; may be a capable bowler who has merely fallen into a slump. The third position exerts the least pressure on a bowler who is not prepared.

   d. Fourth bowler: the well-conditioned strike bowler who likes to attack the pocket aggressively. Striking out in the 10th frame takes a lot of pressure off the next bowler.

   e. Fifth, or *anchor*, bowler: a steady player who can *string* strikes (make many strikes in a row), but who is also a sharp spare shooter. This player is very calm in *clutch* (crucial) situations and can strike under pressure, especially when the player in fourth position makes an error. **Note:** For a 4-member team, remove bowler #2 or #3 from this list, depending on ability. For a 3-member team, remove either bowlers #2 and #3 or #3 and #4.

6. When regulation (competitive) play begins, enter your team lineup on the scoresheet and remain in and around the settee area of your pair of lanes. Help to create a winning atmosphere for your team at all times through your words and actions, which refect the following positive behaviors:

   • Be attentive. Show by your interest that you are ready to bowl and to win. Meet the previous player stepping off of the approach (but remember that you are now in the mental planning phase of your routine). You may have an opportunity to be the hero and get a strike or spare in a clutch situation, but you won't have this opportunity if you don't know how the game is progressing!

   • Be enthusiastic. Act like you "came to play." Motivate your teammates, but be careful how you motivate. Since bowling is an accuracy game (like golf or archery), too much arousal (such as in football or basketball) can interfere with correct movements. Therefore, avoid shouting, hand-slapping, and so on. Don't disturb a teammate when he or she is trying to focus. Limited conversation for the purpose of encouraging or helping a teammate is appropriate during relief time. Do not encroach on yours or your teammates' mental planning time, however, for any type of conversation. In summary, congratulate, motivate, and take care of your team's business, but try to give each bowler on your team the opportunity to concentrate and maintain continuity of performance.

   • Be supportive. Think T-E-A-M-W-O-R-K, and stay involved in the action so you can be available to help your teammates when necessary. Make quick physical adjustments as the lane conditions change, and share your discoveries with your teammates for the good of the team effort. Put extra effort into making a strike or converting a tough spare if your team is bowling a poor frame.

## LEAGUE AND TOURNAMENT SUCCESS STOPPERS

You can increase your chances for success in all types of competition if you learn to diagnose and correct disturbing and distracting behaviors inconsistent with successful competition before they become habitual. The following are only a few examples of such behaviors with some suggested corrections.

| Error | Correction |
|---|---|
| **_Preparation Prior to Competition_** | |
| 1. Hand, fingers and/or thumb constantly sore. | 1. Check for correctness of grip and weight of ball. Correct any discrepancies so you will have plenty of time to practice with the appropriate fit and ball weight before competition. |
| 2. Do not feel well-balanced during the delivery and/or cannot get good leverage at the finish. | 2. Check your shoes. If necessary, put a gum rubber sole on your nonsliding foot. If your heels are too hard (e.g., plastic), get a new pair of shoes with softer rubber heels. |
| 3. Personal items (bowling bag, coat, etc.) strewn over the settees and/or concourse floor. | 3. Stow all personal items in the proper places. Having to move personal items while bowling is disturbing to yourself, as well as being annoying to teammates, competitors, and spectators. |
| 4. Carrying out excessive, unproductive conversation ("visiting") just prior to competition. | 4. After taking care of administrative business (checking in, filling out scoresheets, etc.), begin to focus on your performance. Try to maintain a "cone of focus" until competition is over. |
| 5. Drinking stimulants (coffee, soft drinks) and/or depressants (alcohol) prior to (and during) competition. | 5. Do not alter your senses in any way prior to competition. Drinking coffee and soft drinks that contain caffeine will interfere with the fine movements you need to bowl well under pressure. The use of depressants, such as alcohol, will interfere with shot accuracy, analysis, and planning. |

| Error | Correction |
|---|---|
| **During Competition** | |
| 1. Constant adjustment of the fit of the thumbhole with plastic tape. | 1. The ball's span(s) and/or hole sizes are not correct. Use another ball that fits correctly and adjust the incorrect fit between competitions. |
| 2. Changing the target line too often or in an unsystematic way. | 2. Check for correct execution first. Then, try your favorite target line again, adjusting if necessary using the 3-0-1-2 system. |
| 3. Changing balls too frequently within a game. | 3. Check for correct execution. Changing balls can break concentration; execute correctly first, then change target lines, then change balls only if it is hooking too much or too little or not carrying pins when hitting the pocket consistently. |
| 4. Losing the touch after several successful shots. | 4. Be productive between shots; adhere to the Mental Toughness Routine. |
| 5. Engaging in too much activity (arousal) such as "high fives," etc. while a bowler is returning from his or her shot. | 5. Use the Mental Toughness Routine. Lower the excitement level of motivation of yourself, your lane mates, and your teammates to one that will allow everyone to stay focused. |
| 6. Apparent lack of interest in the match, such as not being ready to bowl a turn, watching television, placing side bets, etc. | 6. Stay on the settee area and pay attention to the progress of the game; use the Mental Toughness Routine. Visit with friends after bowling is finished. |

## LEAGUE AND TOURNAMENT

# DRILLS

### 1. Mental Discipline in a Competitive Game Situation

This drill simulates a highly competitive situation in which you bowl one game against one or more opponents while you are being evaluated by a scorekeeper and an observer. Your two objectives are to outscore your opponent and to adhere faithfully to the Mental Toughness Routine (MTR).

Each bowler bowls in league format. On a pair of lanes, one bowler rolls two balls, then takes his or her seat, allowing the opponents to take two deliveries. Two evaluators are used—one is called the "scorekeeper," and the other is the "observer." The two evaluators will sit together behind the settee area. The bowlers are not allowed to speak with the evaluators once game competition has begun.

**Observer's Tasks**

a. Monitor adherence of all bowlers to the MTR.

b. Assess the "mental lapse penalty" points for any behavior that indicates a lapse in routine.

A lapse is any instance in which the bowler omits or violates one of the requirements of the

MTR. Common lapses include unnecessary contact with opponents, spectators, and evaluators; not sitting down between frames; not taking enough time prior to making a shot; and watching other bowlers. Ten points are subtracted for each lapse.

c. Immediately after each frame, inform the scorekeeper of the number of mental lapse penalty points to be subtracted.

### Scorekeeper's Tasks

a. Record the standard game score for all competitors.

b. Add "ability to recover points" to the final score of the game. These points are added for performance during the first ball of a frame following an open frame:

- 0 points for missing the pocket by more than 3 boards regardless of the results at the pins, including any *crossover hit (Brooklyn)*.
- 5 points for a strike in the pocket and in which the headpin rebounds off the kickboard.
- 10 points for a solid pocket hit (not necessarily a strike) on the first ball after an open frame.

c. Add "difficulty bonus points" to the final score of the game. These points may be added for performance during a frame in which difficult spares were successfully converted:

- 0 points for converting impossible splits due to luck (4-6, 7-9, 8-10, 7-10, 4-6-7-10).
- 5 points for conversion of simple splits in which all pins may be hit with the ball (2-7, 3-10, 4-5, 5-6).
- 10 points for simple splits with a pin added (2-7-10, 2-7-8, 3-7-10, 3-9-10, etc.), *washout* conversions (a headpin and corner pin combination with pins missing between), and kingpin splits (5-7, 5-10).
- 20 points for difficult splits (4-7, 4-9, 4-7-10, 4-7-9-10, 6-7, 6-8, 6-7-10, 6-7-8-10, 4-6-7-8-10, 4-6-7-9-10).

d. Immediately after a bowler has completed a frame, the scorekeeper should write a "+" and the total number of added points in the lower left corner of the frame.

e. The observer should inform the scorekeeper of the number of mental lapse penalty points (details soon) to be subtracted from a frame. Thereupon, the scorekeeper should write a "–" and the total number of subtracted points for both first- and second-ball attempts in the lower right corner of the frame.

f. Each bowler receives a raw scratch score of pins knocked down each game. However, the scorekeeper also calculates the number of points added and subtracted; this sum is added to the bowler's scratch score to obtain a final score.

**Success Goal** = To gain the most game points; use the chart below to record your success:

|  | Raw | Scorekeeper (+) | Observer (–) | Total points |
|---|---|---|---|---|
| Yourself | ____ | ____ | ____ | ____ |
| Opponent #1 | ____ | ____ | ____ | ____ |
| Opponent #2 | ____ | ____ | ____ | ____ |
| Opponent #3 | ____ | ____ | ____ | ____ |

**Success Check**

- Bowl a game against one or more opponents ___
- Be evaluated for adherence to MTR ___

### To Increase Difficulty

- Add distractors to your competition. Have someone try to talk to you and your opponents between shots. Give 10 additional "ability to recover" points for a pocket hit or a spare after such a disturbance.
- Bowl your competition in a crowded, noisy bowling setting.
- Put yourself and your opponents in an actual competitive situation. Bowl against each other in a league or tournament and follow the same procedures as outlined in this drill.

## 2. Match and Medal Play Scoring System

Many protocols (agreed-upon ways) are used in competitive bowling. Many of these protocols involve complex scoring advantage strategies, but it is impossible for you to become familiar with all of these strategies from a brief exposure within a drill. The purposes of some common protocols and the basics of using them follow.

a. *Match versus medal play*: In *match play*, the winner of an individual or team game or series is given one or more points for outscoring the opponent; a 1-pin victory is just as good as a 500-pin victory! Although the score decides who is awarded the points, the actual game score plays no additional part in determining the winner. In *medal play*, pinfall not only determines the winner, but the winner carries pinfall in determining total score for a series of games.

b. *Combination scoring system*: Most professional competition is a combination of match and medal play, with points or pins being awarded for outscoring an opponent in an individual game. Such a system is typical of that used in Professional Bowlers Association tournaments and was derived from the *Peterson Point System*. For example, if two persons bowled a two-game match in which a bowler was awarded 30 points for winning a game, in addition to the number of pins knocked down, the outcome would be as follows:

|  | Game 1 | Game 2 | Total score |
|---|---|---|---|
| Bowler 1 | 225 | 201 | 426 |
| Bowler 2 | 211 | 257 | 468 |

*Calculating point totals*:

Bowler 1 receives 30 points for winning Game 1   426 + 30 = 456
Bowler 2 receives 30 points for winning Game 2   468 + 30 = 498

*Directions*: Bowl two regulation team games against an opposing team using the following match and medal scoring system. Award points like this:

• 30 points to the bowler who outscores the bowler across from him or her in one game.
• 30 points to the bowler who outscores the bowler across from him or her in total pins for two games (optional).
• 30 points to the team who outscores the other team in one game.
• 30 points to the team who outscores the opposing team in total pins for the two games (optional).

**Success Goal** = Complete 2 regulation team games, trying to outscore the opposing team and using the combination match-medal scoring system ___

**Success Check**
• Bowl 2 team games against another team ___
• Add bonus points ___
• Record scores ___

**To Increase Difficulty**
• Put yourself and your opponents in an actual competitive situation. Bowl against each other in a league or tournament and follow the same procedures as outlined in this drill.

**To Decrease Difficulty**
• Bowl only 1 game, adding points to the single-game score.

## 3. Common Team Protocols

Become familiar with the following scoring indexes and lane courtesies:

*Score indexes:* A score index is different from score keeping; it is a means of quickly detecting how far your team is ahead of or behind the opposing team. Two score indexes are kept by tallying either marks (strikes and spares) or misses (open frames) in the little boxes underneath a regulation team scoresheet. In any given team game, one may keep track of either marks or misses, but not both. Either system is very simple.

*Counting marks:* For every bowler who strikes or spares in a frame, one mark is added to the cumulative mark total at the bottom of the scoresheet. A double (two strikes in a row) counts as two marks in the frame where the second strike occurred. If no one on the team gets a strike or spare, no marks are added to the cumulative mark total (see Four-Person Sample Scoresheet).

**Four-Person Sample Scoresheet**

| Name | 1 | 2 | 3 | 4 | 5 | 6 | 7 | 8 | 9 | 10 | Total |
|---|---|---|---|---|---|---|---|---|---|---|---|
| Carol | 9 | 27 | 35 | 53 | 62 | 89 | 109 | 125 | 133 | 149 | 149 |
| Ken | 17 | 35 | 44 | 64 | 93 | 112 | 121 | 139 | 156 | 176 | 325 |
| Joy | 20 | 50 | 78 | 98 | 115 | 133 | 142 | 162 | 190 | 210 | 535 |
| Andy | 9 | 27 | 35 | 53 | 73 | 102 | 122 | 139 | 159 | 177 | 712 |
| (Marks) | 2 | 6 | 8 | 13 | 16 | 21 | 25 | 29 | 32 | 37 | |

*Counting misses:* In this second system, if every bowler strikes or spares in a frame, nothing is added to the cumulative total at the bottom of the scoresheet; the misses are said to be "even." Every double counts as +1 in the frame where the second strike occurred. For every bowler who fails to strike or spare, a –1 is added to the cumulative miss total in the frame where the miss occurred (see Five-Person Sample Scoresheet).

**Five-Person Sample Scoresheet**

| Name | 1 | 2 | 3 | 4 | 5 | 6 | 7 | 8 | 9 | 10 | Total |
|---|---|---|---|---|---|---|---|---|---|---|---|
| Joe | 29 | 49 | 68 | 86 | 106 | 135 | 155 | 175 | 195 | 213 | 213 |
| Helen | 18 | 27 | 53 | 72 | 81 | 99 | 119 | 148 | 167 | 176 | 309 |
| Allen | 30 | 57 | 75 | 83 | 113 | 143 | 169 | 187 | 195 | 223 | 612 |
| Marci | 26 | 45 | 54 | 74 | 91 | 98 | 107 | 126 | 146 | 165 | 777 |
| Phil | 17 | 36 | 45 | 72 | 92 | 112 | 137 | 152 | 179 | 198 | 975 |
| (Misses) | (even) | +2 | +1 | +1 | +1 | +1 | +2 | +3 | +3 | +4 | |

*Lane courtesy:* Lane courtesy refers to the practice of allowing others around you to bowl before you take your setup and delivery. The typical type of courtesy used in most amateur league competition is *one-lane* courtesy. One-lane courtesy requires that you allow only the bowlers ready on the lanes immediately to your right and your left to bowl before you.

Professional and scratch amateur competition often feature *two-lane* or *one-pair* courtesy as an aid to concentration. This practice requires that you allow the bowlers two lanes, or one pair, to your right and left to bowl before you. This way, there are always two unused approaches between bowlers taking their deliveries.

*Changing lanes:* In tournament competition, bowlers are often required to commence bowling on one pair of lanes, then to change lanes, moving to another pair of lanes for the next and subsequent games. This practice allows bowlers to bowl on the same lanes as all others.

In both professional and amateur competition, it is common to (a) move to the next pair of lanes to the right; (b) *skip one* pair, moving two pairs of lanes to the right, for example, going from lanes 3 and 4 to lanes 7 and 8; and (c) *skip two* pairs, moving three pairs of lanes to the right, for example, going from lanes 7 and 8 to lanes 13 and 14. The group bowling on the end pair of lanes would move to an appropriate pair of lanes on the other end of the establishment.

Now, you are ready to bowl two regulation team games against an opposing team, scoring only pinfall. In Game 1, count marks and use one-lane courtesy. Skip two pairs to the right before beginning the next game. In Game 2, count misses and use two-lane courtesy.

**Success Goal** = Complete 2 regulation team games, attempting to outscore the opposing team, and using score indexes and lane courtesy as directed ___

**Success Check**
• Bowl 2 team games against another team ___
• Count marks and misses ___
• Use one-lane and two-lane courtesy ___

**To Increase Difficulty**
• Bowl against each other in a league or tournament in which these common protocols are used.

**To Decrease Difficulty**
• Bowl only 1 game, but use 2 spaces directly underneath each frame to keep both marks and misses.

## 4. Doubles Competition

Learn how to bowl doubles competition in two different formats.

*Scotch doubles* is competition in which two persons participate in bowling a single regulation gameline. Opposing Scotch doubles teams bowl each other on a pair of lanes, alternating lanes each frame. The leadoff bowler bowls the first ball of the first frame, and his or her partner bowls at the spare. In the event that the leadoff bowler strikes, the partner becomes the leadoff bowler in the next frame. Thus, frame leadoff honors change every time a strike is rolled.

*Best-ball doubles* is slightly different. Two persons participate in bowling a single regulation gameline, but both partners get up to bowl at the same time, each on one lane of the pair; partners alternate the lanes on which they bowl each frame. The partner on the left lane of the pair (leadoff bowler) always bowls first, while the other partner (anchor bowler) waits. If the leadoff bowler rolls a strike, both partners sit down, allowing the other team to bowl. The strike is scored in the appropriate frame of their gameline.

If the best-ball team's leadoff partner does not strike, the anchor partner has a chance to roll a better pin count for score. If the anchor bowler knocks down more pins *without leaving a more difficult spare*, then the anchor bowler finishes the frame, and the score for that frame is posted. If partners match pin count, they discuss their options, usually electing the partner with the less difficult spare to roll for score. However, if the anchor bowler has knocked down fewer pins *with a less difficult spare*, then he or she will probably finish the frame. Regardless of the results, the score of this partner will be posted. The other partner will sweep off the remaining pins, setting a full rack for the opposing team.

Bowl two doubles games against opponents. Bowl one game in the Scotch doubles format and the other in best-ball doubles format. Record your scores below.

**Success Goal** = Complete 2 doubles games against opponents, one game in Scotch doubles format, the other in best-ball doubles format; use the following chart to keep track of your game scores ___

**Success Check**
- Bowl 2 doubles games against opponents ___
- Use both doubles formats ___

**To Increase Difficulty**
- Use 1- or 2-lane courtesy and skip 1 or 2 pairs of lanes after each game.
- Add 75% of the difference between the averages of the two doubles teams to the lower-average team's score (see Drill 8, p. 153). Then add Peterson Points to each game score.

**To Decrease Difficulty**
- Bowl only 1 game, picking either format to bowl.

## 5. Fostering Team Spirit

The creation and maintenance of a positive team atmosphere is essential to winning.

a. Each team member should read and check off the recommendations below, resolving to cooperate in bringing them about for the good of the team.

*Team Goal:* To win through superior performance and good sportsmanship

*Team Captain Directions:* Put a check to indicate your individual goals in pursuit of the team goal.

___ To treat all others fairly
___ To understand and carry out my duties effectively
___ To make optimum use of the team lineup

- First bowler: most consistent
- Second bowler: steady and a good spare shooter
- Third bowler: least consistent or lowest average
- Fourth bowler: aggressive strike bowler
- Fifth bowler: steady clutch bowler

___ To ensure that all fees are paid in full in a timely manner

*Individual Team Members' Directions:* Put a check mark under your team lineup number to indicate that you have studied this drill. Check off your individual goals in pursuit of the team goal underneath your team lineup number.

| | | Member number | | | |
|---|---|---|---|---|---|
| | 1 | 2 | 3 | 4 | 5 |

**At all times:**

— — — — — To be committed to the team goals
— — — — — To help my team attain excellence
— — — — — To help my team exhibit good sportsmanship
— — — — — To be reliable
— — — — — To actively maintain a harmonious attitude
— — — — — To show concern for others
— — — — — To praise others sincerely
— — — — — To be supportive and motivational
— — — — — To give advice when appropriate

**During practice:**

— — — — — To help my teammates line up

**During competition:**

— — — — — To remain in the settee area
— — — — — To follow my Mental Toughness Routine
— — — — — To pay attention at all times
— — — — — To be ready to bowl each frame
— — — — — To be an enthusiastic teammate
— — — — — To be an encouraging teammate
— — — — — To bowl to the best of my ability
— — — — — To control my temper
— — — — — To make quick physical adjustments
— — — — — To try harder when behind

b. Now bowl three regulation team games, competing against an opposing team for score. Each team member should always act in a manner reflecting pursuit of the goals above.

**Success Goal** = Complete 3 regulation team games, attempting to outscore the opposing team while pursuing your individual and unified team goals ___

**Success Check**
- Bowl 3 team games ___
- Adhere to the recommendations in this drill ___
- Try to reach the team goal ___

**To Increase Difficulty**
- Add handicap to the scores (see Drill 8, p. 153), count marks and/or misses, use the appropriate lane courtesy, and add points for winning the game.
- Have an observer keep notes on each member's performance and make them available to each performer after each game.

**To Decrease Difficulty**
- Bowl only 1 or 2 games.

## 6. Corner Pin Derby and Relay

This is a fast-paced, challenging game that enhances group cohesiveness. It involves all bowlers rolling at only the 7 and 10 pins. The Derby is singles competition, while the Relay is team competition. The larger the group of bowlers, the more appropriate is the Relay.

*Derby rules*: All competition begins on lane 1. The first competitor rolls at either the 7 or the 10 pin on lane 1. If successful in picking up only the single pin, he or she moves on to lane 2 and again rolls at either the 7 or 10 pin, while the next competitor rolls at the remaining corner pin from the first competitor's first attempt (this eliminates the necessity of respotting pins). All competitors follow along behind in the same manner.

*Objective*: To stay in the competition. A competitor is out if he or she rolls a ball in the channel or hits any pins other than the 7 or the 10 pin. A competitor is "home free" after 10 consecutive successful attempts. After all competitors are home free or called out, the competition begins another round, this time among only home-free competitors. The competition ends when all but one competitor has been called out. This single, remaining home-free (sharpshooting) bowler is designated the winner.

*Relay variation*: Designate teams of two or more persons each before competition begins. The leadoff bowler of each team begins on lane 1 and proceeds as in the Derby, followed by the leadoff bowler of the next team.

When the leadoff bowler of a team is declared out, the second member of the team replaces the leadoff bowler, beginning his or her competition on the lane following the one where the leadoff bowler was declared out. A team is out of competition when the last bowler on the team has been declared out; a team member has only one chance in the competition. After all teams have either made it home free or have been called out, the competition begins another round, this time among only the home-free team representatives. The competition ends when all but one team has been called out. This team is then designated the winner.

**Success Goal** = Stay in the competition as long as possible ___

**Success Check**
- Bowl the derby or relay competition ___
- Use your best execution and targeting skills ___

**To Increase Difficulty**
- Require right-handers to knock down the 7 pin first and left-handers to knock down the 10 pin.

**To Decrease Difficulty**
- Require all competitors to knock down a minimum number of pins to avoid being called out. A minimum of 6 pins makes the drill much less difficult.
- Allow 2 or more outs per bowler before being called out.

### 7. Bowling Golf

This drill combines the golf concept of shooting par with strike-and-spare skills. Each "golfer" uses a single regulation bowling gameline but does not keep a regulation bowling score. Ten "holes," or frames, constitute a round of Bowling Golf. Scoring is as follows:

- Double Strike: A strike after a previous strike is an "eagle," or "two under par" for the frame in which the second strike is scored. This scoring represents a bonus; no additional bonus is given for 3 or more strikes.
- Strike: The score is a "birdie," "one under par," or "minus one" for the frame.
- Spare: The score for the frame is "even" or "par."
- Miss: Leaving one pin standing after two balls is a "bogey," "one over par," or "plus one"; leaving two standing is a "double bogey"; leaving three standing is a "triple bogey," and so on.
- Converting a Split: Converting any split to a spare is a "birdie," or "minus one."

*Rules*: Competition is on either a single lane or on a pair. If there are fewer than three persons assigned to a lane, the bowlers on a pair of lanes play against each other and alternate lanes. If more, bowlers on each lane compete among themselves on a single lane.

*Sample scoring for three bowlers*: The leadoff bowler starts the action with a strike (birdie); the score for his or her first frame is –1. The second bowler rolls his or her first frame, rolling a seven count and knocking down only one pin on the second attempt (double bogey); the score in the first frame is +2. The third bowler rolls next, getting a split that is converted into a spare (birdie); the resulting score is a –1.

In the second frame, the leadoff bowler gets another strike (an eagle), the second bowler gets a strike, and the third bowler gets a strike. In the third frame, the leadoff bowler gets a split and "eight out" (leaving two pins standing); the second bowler gets a spare; and the third bowler gets another strike. The score so far:

| Bowler | 1 | 2 | 3 | Cumulative Total |
|---|---|---|---|---|
| Leadoff | – 1 | – 2 | +2 | – 1 |
| Second | +2 | – 1 | even | + 1 |
| Third | – 1 | – 1 | -2 | – 4 |

The third bowler is in the lead, three "strokes" ahead of the leadoff bowler and five strokes ahead of the second bowler.

### Success Goal =

a. Complete 1 round of Bowling Golf, attempting to make the lowest score ___
b. Skins game: complete 1 round of golf, attempting to accumulate the greatest number of points ___

### To Increase Difficulty

- *Skins game variation*: Award 5 points to the winner of an individual hole (frame). In case of a tie for hole winner, carry over the 5 points, adding them to the 5 winner's points on the next hole.

### Success Check

- Normal delivery ___
- Use correct strike-targeting technique ___
- Use correct spare-targeting technique ___
- Try to strike and spare ___
- Score birdies, pars, and bogeys ___

## 8. Handicap Scoring Exercise

If you bowl with or against persons of unequal ability, a *handicap* will probably be added to the *raw*, or *scratch*, score of the bowler(s) with less skill (lower average). Adding handicaps is an attempt to equalize the winning chances of all bowlers in a group (a "field").

There are many ways to determine a handicap for a bowler; none is particularly valid or reliable. However, there are two popular methods. When handicapping with the *percentage difference* method, you subtract bowler B's score from bowler C's score, and 70, 80, or 90 percent of the difference between the scores of two bowlers (or teams) represents the handicap. (If more than one person is bowling, each bowler's average is subtracted from the highest average in the group.) With the *percentage from base score* method, you assume some arbitrary *base score*, such as 200, 210, or 220. Then each bowler's average score is subtracted from the base score and multiplied by a percentage (usually 70, 80, or 90 percent) to get a handicap.

To learn how to add handicap to a bowler's score, let's assume that three bowlers of unequal ability bowled one game against the other two.

The <u>averages</u> of the bowlers are:     Bill = 135, Sally = 118, and Ned = 191

The <u>raw scores</u> of the games are:     Bill = 157, Sally = 143, and Ned = 206

Using the handicapping methods explained above, figure what handicap scores (raw score plus handicap) each of the bowlers would have and make a statement as to who is the winner in each case. Give yourself one point for each correctly calculated handicap, one point for each correctly calculated handicap score, and one point for correctly naming the winner in each case; the total number of points for this drill is 14 (7 points if you choose only one method).

### Percentage Difference Method
**(90% in this example)**

(Hint: Ned, having the highest average in the group, would get no handicap. With the 90%, Ned theoretically would have a 10% edge over the others in the group.)

Bill     157 + ___ = ____

Sally     143 + ___ = ____

Ned     206 + ___ = ____

Winner: _____

### Percentage from Base Score Method
**(80% from a 220 base score in this example)**

(Hint: All bowlers would receive handicap.)

Bill     157 + ___ = ____

Sally     143 + ___ = ____

Ned     206 + ___ = ____

Winner: _____

**Don't** look at the answers on the next page until you have tried to do the drill!

### To Increase Difficulty

• Use both methods in an actual competitive setting in which more than two bowlers compete; refigure each person's average after each game (keep a "running average") and recalculate the handicaps before the next game begins.

• Keep score for 2 teams of bowlers, calculating scores and handicaps from previous individual running averages. Then use team scores as the raw scores to which handicaps are added.

### To Decrease Difficulty

• Use only 1 method to calculate handicap (7 possible points).

### Answers for the Percentage Difference Method

We will try to give handicap based on each bowler's average in relation to the highest average in the group—in this case, Ned, with a 191 average, is the base score from which handicaps are calculated.

Handicap Calculation: Bill's average is 135

Bill's handicap is 191 − 135 = 56; 56 × .90 = 50.4—rounded off to 50 pins

Sally's average is 118

Sally's handicap is 191 − 118 = 73; 73 × .90 = 65.7—rounded off to 66 pins

Ned's average is 191

Ned's handicap is 191 − 191 = 0; 0 × .90 = 0

Handicap Score Calculation:
Bill    157 + 50 = 207
Sally   143 + 66 = 209
Ned     206 +  0 = 206

With this method, Sally is the winner of the game.

### Answers for the Percentage From Base Score Method

(80% from a 220 base score in this example)

Handicap Calculation: Bill's average is 135

Bill's handicap is 220 − 135 = 85; 85 × .80 = 68 pins

Sally's average is 118

Sally's handicap is 220 − 118 = 102; 102 × .80 = 81.6 rounded off to 82 pins

Ned's average is 191

Ned's handicap is 220 − 191 = 29; 29 × .90 = 26.1 rounded off to 26 pins

Handicap Score Calculation:
Bill    157 + 68 = 225
Sally   143 + 82 = 225
Ned     206 + 26 = 232

With this method, Ned is the winner.

Are you surprised that changing the handicap system used may also change the winner—even though the bowlers' averages and scratch scores remained the same?

## LEAGUE AND TOURNAMENT SUCCESS SUMMARY

No matter whether you choose to compete at a recreational, social, or tournament level, or choose not to compete at all, you can have a lot of fun and rewarding experiences through bowling and meeting other bowlers. It may take you a while to see the benefit from what you have learned in this step, but as you grow in experience, just keep refining your skills—both mental and physical. Doing your best will give more satisfaction, so use this book as a refresher whenever needed. Have fun bowling!

# RATING YOUR PROGRESS

After completing the steps in this book, it is time to evaluate your progress. There are four important areas to self-assess: background knowledge, physical skills, mental skills, and attitude.

## Background Knowledge

Do you feel comfortable around other bowlers and in conversation with bowlers of all skill levels? Rate yourself objectively on your working knowledge of the following concepts associated with bowling. Write either "yes" or "no" in the blank.

**Do you know**

how bowling emerged as a competitive sport? ___

the relative dimensions of the approach, the lane, and related bowling equipment? ___

the meaning of bowling terms as defined in the glossary? ___

how to keep score, including score index? ___

Responses other than "yes" tell you to review and study the corresponding concepts. If all of your checks are in the "yes" category, congratulations! This indicates your potentially high level of confidence in a bowling environment!

## Physical Skills

Do you feel that you have an effective physical game? Rate yourself honestly on the following physical skills using the best one of four responses: excellent, good, average, or poor.

Executing the setup and the four-step delivery _____

Rolling effective straight and hook balls _____

Targeting effectively for strikes _____

Targeting effectively for spares _____

Practicing effectively _____

Responses other than "excellent" tell you to work on the corresponding items. Congratulations if you got all excellent ratings!

## Mental Skills

Do you maintain effective mental control in game situations? Rate yourself honestly on the following mental skills; assume that all statements apply only to competitive bowling. Use any one of five responses: always, sometimes, seldom, never, or unaware.

Setting realistic performance goals that lead to improvement _____

Avoiding tendency to tense up _____

Controlling my anger quickly _____

Sustaining a high level of concentration _____

Using a progressive muscle relaxation technique _____

Making positive self-statements _____

Visualizing myself making perfect shots before I make an actual shot _____

Talking only when necessary _____

   Responses other than "always" indicate that you should work on the corresponding skills. Congratulations if you rated yourself "always" on all items. You are in control!

## Attitude

Do you gain true satisfaction from bowling? Rate your present attitude toward bowling by responding to the following statements. Select from the previous five response options.

Looking forward to my next bowling session _____

Believing that bowling is only an extension of myself, not having a bowling obsession _____

Studying bowling between sessions_____

Mentally practicing between sessions _____

Keeping a record of all of my scores _____

Talking about bowling with others _____

Helping other bowlers when asked to do so _____

Believing that my performance will steadily improve through my own application and effort _____

Feeling that I may experience something new at my next bowling session _____

Feeling that I may beat my previous best performances during my next bowling session _____

   Responses other than "always" indicate some degree of confusion or dissatisfaction with the corresponding aspect of bowling. Congratulations if you now derive satisfaction and enjoyment from bowling!

# APPENDIX: SCORESHEET

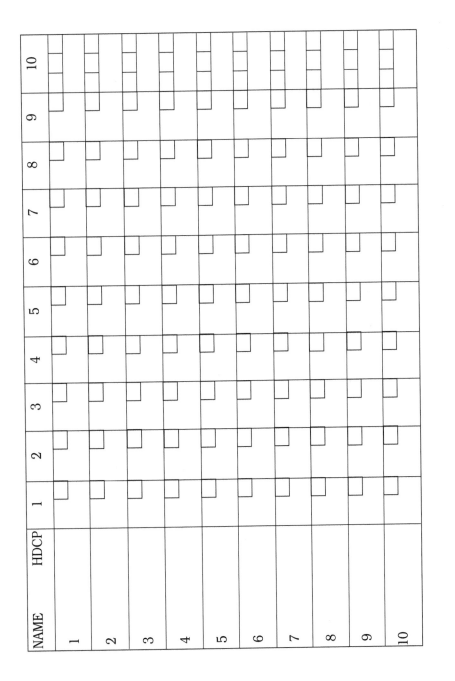

# GLOSSARY

**action**—Movement of a body part; also the movement of the pins after ball impact.

**address**—Stance position; see **setup**.

**alignment**—Positioning of the swing or approach relative to a target or a line.

**alley**—Playing surface for bowling.

**angle of attack**—Angle at which the ball rolls into the rack of pins.

**approach**—Taking steps and swinging the ball during the delivery; area on which a bowler takes steps in delivering the ball.

**approach line**—Line over which the center of the body moves during the approach.

**axis of rotation**—Line through the center of the ball, around which the ball rotates while rolling.

**backswing**—Portion of the swing starting at the lowest point in the downswing and ending with the ball at its highest point behind the bowler.

**backup ball**—Ball that veers from the bowler's inside to the outside.

**balance arm**—Arm opposite the bowling (swingside) arm.

**balance side**—Portion of the bowler's body, the lane, or the approach on the same side as the nonbowling (balance) arm.

**ball track**—Area on the surface of a bowling ball over which it rolls; area on the lane surface where frequent ball contact causes wear.

**base score**—Arbitrary score from which handicap may be calculated.

**be snooty**—Keeping the head back, looking at visual target out of the bottoms of the eyes, and following the visual target only with the eyes, not with the head.

**bowling hand** or **arm**—Hand or arm with which the bowler rolls the ball.

**break point**—Location down the lane at which a bowler's ball visibly begins to hook.

**Brooklyn**—Refers to the strike ball; a hit on the side of the headpin opposite the bowling hand.

**bumpout swing**—Backswing that moves away from the center of the body.

**carry**—Extent to which a ball tends to strike; also knocking down a particular pin, for example, to carry the 7 pin.

**channel**—Trough, or gutter, on each side of a lane.

**checkpoint**—Each characteristic evaluated in a check sequence.

**check sequence**—Orderly series of checks performed on any system; for example, checks on the setup, the steps, the grip.

**chop**—To knock down the front pins in a spare leave while leaving the back pins standing.

**clear**—Term specifically applied to the fingers during the release of the ball; exiting the grip hole without restriction.

**clip**—Stopping the ball on its way to the top of the backswing.

**conventional grip**—Ball grip in which both fingers are inserted to the second joints.

**convergent swing**—Swing plane directed toward the front center of the bowler.

**convert**—Knocking down all pins left standing after the first-ball attempt of a frame; making a spare.

**cover**—To make a spare; to hit all pins of a spare leave with the ball; the outside layer in a bowling ball's construction.

**curve ball**—A shot that travels a curved path to the pins from the bowler's outside to the inside but which shows no definite break point.

**delivery**—Rolling the ball down the lane.

**divergent swing**—Swing plane directed toward the front outside of the bowler.

**downswing**—Portion of the bowler's swing starting at the extended pushaway position and

ending with the ball at its lowest point as it is moving back.

**dumped shot**—Lack of finger lift in delivering the ball, usually caused by the ball being early relative to the footwork.

**dynamics**—Collective movement of objects in motion.

**early pushaway**—Pushaway of the ball occurring before movement of the swingside foot.

**error**—Failure of frame's second ball to knock down all the pins left standing by the first ball; performance of an action other than that desired.

**extension setup**—Ball being held at the extended pushaway position.

**fast feet**—Steps being taken at a pace faster than the cadence of the pendulum swing.

**fast lane**—A low-friction lane on which it is difficult to roll a hook ball.

**find a line**—To systematically adjust the target line and stance position until the ball is hitting the pocket.

**finger inserts**—Plastic or rubber liners within the fingerholes, which allow a snug fit and greater traction.

**fingers in the shot**—Feeling the fingers lift the ball, imparting roll or rotation at the release.

**fingertip**—Ball grip in which both fingers are inserted to the first joints.

**finish**—Last-step-and-slide stage of the delivery.

**following the ball down**—Leaning the torso forward as the ball is moving into the downswing.

**forward swing**—Portion of the bowler's swing starting at the top of the backswing and ending at the release point.

**foul**—Any part of the bowler's body touching any part of the bowling establishment beyond the foul line during an otherwise legal delivery of the ball.

**foul line**—Line that separates the approach from the lane.

**frame**—Unit division of a game of bowling that allows for two attempts at knocking down a full rack of pins.

**full-roller**—Ball that bears a track equal to its full circumference.

**grip, proper**—Curling the fingers while keeping the thumb straight and pressing the straightened thumb in the direction of the fingers; there should be no bending of the thumb at the first joint.

**handicap**—Pins added in an attempt to equalize one bowler's score with another's.

**headpin**—Pin at the front of the rack of pins.

**high hit**—Ball contacts the front pin of a full rack or a spare combination too fully.

**hoist**—"Adding to" the pendulum action of the backswing with muscular tension, resulting in a higher than desired backswing.

**hook ball**—Shot that follows a bent path to the pins from the bowler's outside to the inside.

**hooking lane**—Lane with a high-friction condition.

**illegal pinfall**—Pinfall resulting from any of the following: a ball which has left the lane surface before reaching the pins, a ball rebounding from the rear cushion, pins knocked down but returning to a standing position, pins touched by the pinsetter before they fall.

**impact board**—Specific term referring to the lane board number over which the ball rolled as it made contact with the pins.

**impact point**—General term denoting the point of ball contact with the pins.

**inside**—Portion of the bowler's body, the lane, or the approach that is on the same side as the balance arm; see **balance side**.

**kickboard**—Wall on either side of the rack of pins, from which they can rebound.

**kingpin**—5 pin.

**lane condition**—State of friction of the lane.

**lane courtesy**—Protocol in which bowlers on adjacent lanes or lane pairs may take orderly turns in rolling balls.

**lane dressing**—Oil applied over the lane finish to reduce wear by the ball.

**lane finish**—Tough plastic (urethane, lacquer, etc.) coating applied to seal and protect the bare lane surface.

**late pushaway**—Pushaway of the ball occurring after movement of the swingside foot has already begun.

**league**—Form of organized competition, with winners usually determined at the end of a 9-month bowling season.

**leave**—Any pins left standing after the first-ball attempt in a frame.

**legal delivery**—Ball leaves the bowler's hand and touches the lane past the foul line.

**lift**—To impart roll or rotation to a bowling ball with the bowling fingers.

**light hit**—Any first-ball attempt in which the ball barely touches the headpin to the outside.

**line bowling**—Aiming method that uses an imaginary line.

**locking the elbow**—A low-stress 180-degree extension of the arm(s) after a decisive, continuous, but non-thrusting movement of the ball from the setup position to the final pushaway destination.

**loft**—To deliver a ball too far out onto the lane surface, usually caused by bending the thumb in the thumbhole.

**low friction**—Relative term describing a tendency for two touching surfaces to slide over each other easily.

**make**—To knock down all pins standing; one makes a strike or a spare.

**mark**—Either a spare or a strike, all 10 pins being knocked down in a frame.

**match play**—Competitive event in which the winner is determined by number of games won, not by the game scores.

**medal play**—Competitive event in which the winner is determined by game scores.

**mental imagery**—Willful, detailed imagining of persons, places, events, sensations, feelings.

**mental practice**—Repetitious rehearsal of an activity in the mind.

**midline ball setup**—Holding the ball at waist-level with both hands.

**miss**—See **error**.

**negative axis pole**—End of ball's axis of rotation farther away from the headpin; the outside pole.

**next-up position**—Recommended body position and location taken immediately before stepping up onto the approach.

**one-step delivery**—Exercise used by a bowler to practice the last-step-and-slide stage of the delivery.

**opening up**—Movement of the bowling shoulder toward the back, away from the target.

**open play**—Unscheduled, casual bowling.

**outside**—Portion of the bowler's body, the lane, or the approach on the same side as the bowling arm; see **swingside**.

**overlearn**—To drill on a procedure until it becomes automatic.

**parallel line bowling**—Targeting system involving a logical relationship between the ball path and the path of the footwork.

**pendulum**—Weight suspended from a fixed point and swinging freely under only the action of gravity.

**percentage difference handicap**—Number of pins added to the score of the lower-average bowler based on the difference between his or her average and that of the bowler being competed against.

**percentage from base score handicap**—Number of pins added to the score of a bowler based on the difference between his or her average and a base score, for example, 200, 210, 220, and so on.

**pick up**—See **make**.

**pin action**—Movement of the pins after ball impact.

**pin bowling**—Using the pins as a visual target during the delivery.

**pin count**—Number of pins knocked down.

**pindeck**—Area of the lane on which the rack of 10 pins is set.

**pinfall**—Pins knocked down.

**pitch**—Amount of deviation of the axis of a hole away from or toward the geometric center of the ball.

**placement distance**—Distance in boards between the approach line and the target line, or between the body's center of gravity and the plane of the swing.

**playing lanes**—Adjustment of the target line to keep the ball impact point at the strike pocket.

**pocket**—Desired point of ball impact for a strike; the 17th board.

**pocket spare**—Any spare leave which can be made using the strike ball target line.

**positive axis pole**—End of the

ball's axis of rotation closer to the headpin; the inside pole.

**progressive relaxation**—Systematic procedure for willfully relaxing the body.

**projection**—Lifting the ball up and out and onto the lane surface with the fingers.

**pulled shot**—Too much lift in delivering the ball, usually caused by a late ball.

**pushaway**—Horizontal movement of the ball from its position in the setup to the pushaway destination.

**pushaway destination**—Location in the swing plane that allows both elbows to be locked and the ball to be moved horizontally from its setup location—never down.

**push the ball**—To push the ball straight out in the pushaway so that both elbows are locked; the bowling arm is thus completely straight before the ball moves down into the swing.

**rack of pins**—All 10 pins set in a regulation tenpin formation.

*Rangefinders*—Collective system of dots and arrows on the approach and lane.

**raw score**—Actual score of a game before handicap or points are added.

**release**—Letting go of the ball during the slide, preferably with the thumb first, followed by the fingers.

**reverse hook**—Ball that veers from the bowler's inside to the outside; see **backup ball**.

**rolling**—Rotation around a horizontal axis, along a vertical plane; end-over-end motion of the ball proceeding in the direction of the pins; a rolling ball moves forward exactly 27 inches in a single revolution.

**rotation**—Movement of any mass moving around an axis; for example, roll, spin.

**rounding off the pushaway**—Failure to completely push the ball horizontally into the swing plane.

**runway**—Portion of the lane on which the steps are taken; the approach.

**Scotch doubles**—Two-person team competition in which one bowler bowls the first ball of a frame and the partner bowls the second.

**scratch**—Score to which no handicap or points are added; a raw score.

**semiroller**—Ball that bears a track approximately two thirds of the circumference of the ball.

**settee**—Seating area behind each pair of lanes.

**setup**—Phase of the delivery before initiation of movement.

**setup area**—General location on the approach in which the setup is taken.

**shot**—See **delivery**.

**shuffling steps**—Failure to lift the feet sufficiently high off of the approach during the delivery.

**sitting tall**—Ideal finish position at the foul line, keeping the back upright (no more than 20 degrees of forward lean) while the hips are lowered by bending the knees.

**skidding**—Slipping motion of a ball as it proceeds toward the pins; a skidding ball moves forward more than 27 inches in a single revolution.

**slick lane**—Low-friction lane on which the ball tends not to hook.

**sliding foot**—Foot on the side opposite the swing.

**slow lane**—High-friction lane on which the ball hooks readily.

**span**—Distance between the edges of the thumbhole and a fingerhole.

**spare**—Second ball's knocking down all pins left standing after the first-ball attempt of a frame; designated by a slash (/) on the scoresheet.

**spin**—Rotation around a vertical axis; along a horizontal plane.

**spinner**—Ball that bears a track that is one third or less of the circumference of the ball.

**split**—Pins, other than the headpin, left standing with pins missing in between after the first-ball attempt; designated by an open circle on the scoresheet.

**spot bowling**—Use of a point on the lane as a visual target.

**stance**—See **setup**.

**stay behind the ball**—To keep the hand behind the ball and in line with the plane of the swing.

**stay down**—To keep down the hips, not the head, in the finish; see **sitting tall**.

**straight ball**—Ball that travels a straight path to the pins.

**strike**—Knocking down all 10 pins with the first-ball attempt in a frame; designated by an X on the scoresheet.

**supporting fingers**—Fingers on the bowling hand that are not put into the grip holes.

**sweep bar**—Bar on the pinsetting machine that pulls the pins into the area behind the pindeck.

**swing plane**—Entire area bounded by the path of a bowler's swing; it may be termed a *solid circle*.

**swingside**—Portion of the bowler's body, the lane, or the approach on the same side as the bowling arm; see **outside**.

**swingside arm** or **hand**—Arm or hand with which the bowler rolls the ball.

**takeaway**—Moving the balance arm out, back, and down from the pushaway destination at the same speed as the ball.

**target-line bowling**—Targeting system involving two points of reference for a desired ball path and an appropriate path for the footwork to ensure delivery of the ball over the two points.

**target point**—Desired place where the ball rolls across the arrows.

**targeting system**—Orderly procedure for aligning the body with a desired ball path.

**test target line**—Any known target line along which a ball is rolled to test the hooking characteristic of a lane.

**topweight**—Weight added during manufacturing to an undrilled bowling ball to balance the ball after the holes are drilled.

**touchdown**—Place on the lane surface where the ball makes initial contact during the delivery; the first point designated along a target line.

**touchdown point**—Place where the ball should cross the foul line.

**tournament**—Organized competition among bowlers, with winners usually determined at the end of a single event.

**translate a spare**—To envision any spare leave as a simpler one.

**trial swing**—Swinging a ball to test it for appropriate weight.

**visual target**—Place on the lane on which to fix the gaze during the delivery.

**washout**—Headpin and other pins left standing after the first ball of a frame, with pins missing between them.

**wraparound swing**—Backswing that moves toward the center of the body.

# REFERENCES

Allen, G. (1986). *The bowling industry study.* Tempe, AZ: Tempe Publishers.

Allen, G., & Ritger, D. (1981). *The complete guide to bowling strikes.* Tempe, AZ: Tempe Publishers.

Jacobson, E. (1930). *Progressive relaxation.* Chicago: University of Chicago Press.

Powers, W., & Strickland, R. (1996). *Bowling tough: 3 simple methods to improve your performance under pressure.* Duncanville, TX: Professional Sports Services.

Ritger, D., & Allen, G. (1978). *The complete guide to bowling spares.* Tempe, AZ/River Falls, WI: Ritger Sports.

Strickland, R. (1980). *Perceptive bowling.* Duncanville, TX: Professional Sports Services.

Weber, D., & Alexander, R. (1981). *Weber on bowling.* Englewood Cliffs, NJ: Prentice-Hall.

# ABOUT THE AUTHOR

A bowler since 1958, Robert H. (Bob) Strickland won the first of his many championships in 1961. In 1978 he joined the Professional Bowlers Association; five years later he began teaching the sport professionally.

In addition to teaching bowling and pro-shop management skills in 10 countries, Bob writes about the sport: He is the author of *Perceptive Bowling* and has been a guest columnist for the *National Bowlers Journal*. He and his wife, Sue, publish the journal *The Perceptive Bowling Professional*.

In 1986 Bob established the "Perceptive Bowling Clinic Successful Performance" course—a team-taught, comprehensive, and concentrated course for bowlers, pro-shop professionals, trainers, and coaches. He offers private bowling instruction and conducts seminars and workshops on various aspects of the sport, from youth coaching to bowling-center marketing. Bob is a certified Young American Bowling Alliance Coach/Instructor and a member of the Bowling Writers Association of America, World Bowling Writers, and the Sigma Xi honorary research fraternity.

Born in San Mateo, California, Bob grew up in Dallas, Texas, and earned degrees from the University of Texas at Arlington and the University of Georgia. Bob and his wife live in Duncanville, Texas, where he is self-employed as a technical writer and marketing consultant. In his leisure time, Bob enjoys music and reading.